1000

D0053141

CALIFORNIA PLACE NAMES

Their Origin and Meaning

By ERWIN G. GUDDE

UNIVERSITY OF CALIFORNIA PRESS

BERKELEY, LOS ANGELES, AND LONDON

University of California Press
Berkeley and Los Angeles
California

University of California Press, Ltd.
London, England

© 1947, 1949, 1959 by
The Regents of the University of California

Third Revised Edition

ISBN: 0-520-01432-4

9   10   11   12   13   14   15

Manufactured in the United States of America

1000
CALIFORNIA PLACE NAMES

Preface

THIS LITTLE BOOK presents in convenient form the stories behind the names of California counties, cities, rivers, lakes, mountains, bays, and some less important topographical features which arouse the traveler's or reader's interest. Geographical names are part of our language and reflect the history of our State, its social and economic development, its flora and fauna, its connection with the history of our nation, and the psychology of its people. Almost everyone is at least mildly interested in the meaning and origin of our names and the way in which they were applied.

The booklet is based on the second printing (1962) of the second edition, revised and enlarged, of the etymological-geographical dictionary, *California Place Names*. It contains, of course, only a small fraction of the many thousands of place names in the State. In making this selection, care has been taken to include all the important names and such minor ones as are of historical interest, or have a good story behind them, or are typically Californian. The choice of the editor and that of the reader may not always coincide. All suggestions received from observant readers since *1,000 California Place Names* was first published in 1947 have been given careful consideration. I hope that interested readers will continue to send in concrete and constructive criticisms and suggestions.

The names are arranged alphabetically, and each is followed by the name of the county or other territorial unit in which it is situated. N. P. stands for National Park; N. M. for National Monument. When the pronunciation of a name does not follow American phonetic usage, a simple spelling is provided to convey the idea of the way the name is spoken locally. For words of Spanish or other foreign origin the local (not the dictionary) meaning is indicated. Persons whose names are preserved in geographical names are briefly identified. Omitted, for lack of information, are many interesting names which appear on maps or are known locally.

Since this popular edition is based entirely upon *California Place Names,* it was thought advisable not to clutter it with the listing of sources and the acknowledgment of the assistance received from hundreds of my fellow Californians. Students of California history and geography who desire fuller information are referred to the larger work.

However, the names of certain persons and agencies repeatedly quoted in the text may properly be listed here:

Aztec. Many California names can be traced to pre-Mexican dialects.

Bancroft. H. H. Bancroft's *History of California* contains in Volumes II to V a pioneer register which identifies many persons mentioned in the book.

Bidwell. John Bidwell, an important pioneer in northern California after 1841, bestowed a number of names, especially in the Sacramento Valley.

Cabrillo. Juan Rodriguez Cabrillo, a Portuguese navigator in Spanish service, was the first white man to sail along the coast of California (1542).

Coast Survey. The U. S. Coast and Geodetic Survey is in charge of the survey of the coasts of the United States and has been responsible for the application of many place names.

Costanso. Miguel Costanso was the engineer of the Portolá expedition of 1769 and constructed an important map.

Crespi. Padre Juan Crespi was a member and chronicler of the Portolá expedition.

Davidson. George Davidson, who was in charge of the Coast Survey on the Pacific Coast, 1850–1860 and 1868–1895, is responsible for the application of many names along the ocean shore.

Fages. Pedro Fages, a lieutenant of the Portolá expedition, composed an important description of California in 1775.

Font. Padre Pedro Font was chaplain of Anza's second expedition (1775–1776) and left two diaries and some maps.

Frémont. John Charles Frémont was in California in 1843–1844 while on his second western exploring expedition. He again came to California in 1845 and took a prominent part in its acquistion by the United States.

Geographic Board. The U. S. Board on Geographical Names is the final authority on place names in the United States.

Geological Survey. One of the chief activities of the U. S. Geological Survey is the preparation of a topographical atlas of the entire United States. Atlas sheets of quadrangles are published at irregular intervals.

Gregg Party. A party of prospectors led by Dr. Josiah Gregg named many of the rivers between Humboldt and San Francisco bays in the winter of 1849–50.

Jedediah Smith. Most of the place names given by this leader of the first parties (1826 and 1827) to enter California from the Rocky Mountains have not survived.

Land Grant. There were 666 Spanish and Mexican private land grants in what is now the State of California. Many of California's Indian names were preserved in the titles of these grants.

Moraga. Gabriel Moraga in Spanish times led several expeditions into the San Joaquin Valley which applied a number of important names.

Muir. John Muir (1838–1914), famous naturalist and mountaineer, is intimately associated with California nomenclature.

Pacific Railroad Survey. A survey was made in 1853–1854 under the direction of the War Department to ascertain the most practicable route for a railroad to the Pacific Coast.

Palóu. Padre Francisco Palóu was the diarist of the expedition to San Francisco in 1774, founder of the Mission in 1776, biographer of Junípero Serra, and author of *Noticias de la Nueva California.*

Portolá. Gaspar de Portolá led the expedition of 1769 from Baja California to San Francisco Bay.

Preuss. Charles Preuss was cartographer of Frémont's first and second expeditions.

Rancheria is the Spanish name for an Indian village.

Rancho. Unless otherwise stated, a rancho is a farm developed on a land grant.

Vancouver. George Vancouver visited California three times between 1792 and 1794 while in command of a British exploring expedition.

Vizcaíno. Sebastián Vizcaíno, Spanish navigator, explored the coast of what is now the state of California in 1602–1603 and gave several place names which still survive.

Wheeler Survey. Geographical Explorations and Surveys West of the 100th Meridian, 1869–1873, Lieutenant Geo. M. Wheeler in charge.

Whitney Survey. Josiah Dwight Whitney was from 1860 to 1874 in charge of the State Geological Survey.

Wilkes. Charles Wilkes, U.S.N., was in command of an exploring expedition, 1838–1842. Two detachments explored the interior of California in 1841.

The names of some other men connected with place naming in California, such as Sutter, Vallejo, and Muir, are identified in the body of the text.

National Park is abbreviated N. P.; National Monument, N. M.

1,000 California Place Names presents, naturally, only a small fraction of the 150,000 or more geographical names in the state. In making the selection, care was taken to include all important names, like those of the counties, the national domains, the larger cities, the great rivers, the high mountains, the prominent coastal features. In selecting additional less important but interesting names the choice of the author will naturally not always coincide with that of the reader. All additions suggested by observant readers since the publication of the 1947 edition of this little book have been carefully considered.

1,000 California Place Names

Abalone, ab-a-loh'-nee. The name of the large California mollusk, valuable for its meat and its shells, is given to a number of points, rocks, and coves along the coast. The name is of Indian origin and in early American times was spelled *avalone* and *aulone.*

Acalanes, a-ka-lah'-nes [Contra Costa]. The name of a branch of the Costanoan Indians, mentioned as Sacalanes in 1797. The present spelling was used in a land grant of 1834.

Adelanto [San Bernardino]. The Spanish word, meaning 'advance' or 'progress,' is a modern application.

Adobe, a-doh'-bee. The Spanish American term for sun-dried brick occurs frequently in California place names, either because of the composition of the soil or because of the presence of houses built of adobe.

Agassiz, ag'-a-see, **Mount** [Fresno]. In 1879 a peak in the region was named Agassiz Needle, in honor of the Swiss American scientist, Louis Agassiz. Later the name was probably transferred, for the present mountain is not a needle.

Agua, ah'-gwa. The Spanish word for water was frequently used as a generic geographical term for springs, creeks, and ponds. The most common, *agua caliente* for warm springs, has survived in a number of places. Other adjectives used with the term are *amargosa* (bitter), *dulce* (sweet), *fria* (cold), *hedionda* (stinking), *mansa* (gentle), *tibia* (tepid).

Aguanga, a-wahng'-ga [Riverside, San Diego]. An Indian place name, probably a village, mentioned as early as 1821.

Ahwahnee, ah-wah'-nee [Yosemite N. P.]. The original name was probably something like *Ahwahna-chee,* a Yokuts Indian word meaning 'the people of Ahwahna,' i.e., the people who inhabited the deep, grassy valley.

Alabama Hills. *See* Kearsarge.

Alameda, al-a-mee′-da. The name, meaning 'grove of poplar (or cottonwood) trees,' was mentioned in 1794. The name referred later to the creek, was applied to the city by popular vote, and was given to the county by act of the legislature in 1853.

Alamo, al′-a-moh. The Spanish name for poplar or cottonwood is found in the names of creeks, rivers, mountains, and valleys. It is also used for a town in Contra Costa County. Its diminutive form is used in Alamitos Bay [Los Angeles] and elsewhere.

Albany [Alameda]. Named in 1909 after Albany, New York, birthplace of the town's first mayor, Frank J. Roberts.

Albion River [Mendocino]. The ancient name of Britain was applied to the river and a land grant in 1844. In 1579, Francis Drake had landed north of San Francisco and had given the name *Nova Albion* to the country. On many maps the region which is now the State of California was called New Albion until the 19th century.

Alcatraz Island, al′-ka-traz [San Francisco]. The name *Isla de Alcatraces* (pelican island) was given to what is now Yerba Buena Island by Captain Ayala, of the *San Carlos,* in 1775. It was later transferred to the rock, which was for years the site of the federal prison.

Alhambra. The tract in Los Angeles was opened in 1874 and was named for the Moorish palace in Spain, a name made popular by Washington Irving's book. Alhambra Valley in Contra Costa County is a euphonious rendering of the Spanish name *Cañada del Hambre* (valley of hunger).

Aliso, a-lee′-soh. The Spanish name for alder tree was often used for place names in Spanish times and has survived in several districts.

Almaden, al-ma-den′ [Santa Clara]. The quicksilver mine, developed in 1846, was named after the famous mines in Spain. The post office name is now again New Almaden.

Alpine County. Created in 1864 and so named because of its mountainous character.

Alta. The adjective means 'high' in Spanish and is found in many place names. Most of these, such as Altaville, Alta

Loma, Alta Peak, Altamont, were applied in American times. *See* California.

Altadena [Los Angeles]. Coined from *alta* (high) and the last part of Pasa*dena*, because of the town's situation above Pasadena. Applied in 1887.

Alturas [Modoc]. Upon petition of the residents the legislature in 1876 changed the name from Dorrisville to the present Spanish name meaning 'heights.'

Alvarado, al-va-rah′-doh [Alameda]. Named in 1853 for Juan Bautista Alvarado, governor of California, 1836–1842.

Alviso, al-vee′-soh [Santa Clara]. Founded in 1849 and named for Ignacio Alviso, who came as a child with the Anza expedition in 1776 and settled here in 1838.

Amador Valley, am′-a-dohr [Alameda], **Amador County.** José María Amador, a soldier from the San Francisco presidio, settled in the valley in 1826. In 1848 he was successful in mining at the creek which became known by his name. In 1854 the name was applied to the new county.

Amargosa River [Death Valley]. Frémont recorded in April, 1844, that the stream "is called by the Spaniards Amargosa—the bitter-water of the desert."

Amboy [San Bernardino]. The names of the railroad stations from here to the Arizona line were originally (1883) in alphabetical order, named after places "back East": Amboy, Bristol, Cadiz, Danby, Edson, Fenner, Goffs. At a later time, Homer, Ibex (Ibis), and Klinefelter were added.

American River. Sutter derived the name from *El Paso de los Americanos*, the ford where the Canadian trappers, called *Americanos* by Spanish-speaking Indians, crossed the river. Used sporadically before Sutter's coming.

Anacapa Islands [Ventura]. A Chumash Indian word also spelled Anyapah. Vancouver records it as Enneeapah and Enecapah; the present spelling is found on Spanish maps.

Anaheim [Orange]. The "mother colony" of the south, settled by Germans in 1858 and named after the river Santa Ana, plus the suffix *-heim* (home).

Angel Island [San Francisco]. An abbreviation of *Isla de los Angeles,* which had been applied in 1775 by Captain Ayala of the *San Carlos* on or near the date of the day of "Our Lady of the Angels." The Coast Survey chart of 1851 shows it as Los Angeles Island.

Angels Camp [Calaveras]. Next to Coloma probably the oldest still existing mining town in the state. Named for George Angel, of the New York Volunteers in the Mexican War.

Ano Nuevo Point [San Mateo]. The name *Punta de Año Nuevo* was given to the cape by Vizcaíno on January 3, 1603, because it was the first promontory sighted in the new year.

Antioch [Contra Costa]. The name of the Biblical city in Syria was chosen by the inhabitants at a picnic, July 4, 1851.

Anza Desert State Park [San Diego]. Named in 1933 in honor of Juan Bautista de Anza, leader of the famous expedition, which crossed the area in 1774.

Aptos [Santa Cruz]. The name is a Spanish rendering of the Indian name of a rancheria; mentioned in 1807 and applied to a land grant in 1831.

Arbuckle [Colusa]. The railroad station was built in 1875 on the ranch of T. R. Arbuckle, who settled here in 1866.

Arcadia [Los Angeles]. Named in 1888 after the district in Greece, symbolizing in poetry a place of rural simplicity.

Arcata, ar-kay'-ta [Humboldt]. The name, of uncertain Indian origin, was given to the town in 1860.

Arena, a-ree'-na, **Point** [Mendocino]. The cape was known by various names until Vancouver called it *Barro [Barra] de Arena* (sand bar) in 1792.

Arguello, ar-gwel'-loh, **Point** [Santa Barbara]. Named by Vancouver in 1793 for José Dario Argüello, at that time *comandante* at Monterey.

Argus Range [Inyo]. The name of the many-eyed monster of classical mythology was applied to the mining district in 1861.

Aromas [Monterey]. The name is derived from the name of the land grant *Aromitas y Agua Caliente* (little odors and warm water). The *aromas* or *aromitas* referred apparently to the odors of sulphur water.

Arrastre. The Mexican term for the apparatus used to crush ore by dragging heavy weights over it in a circular pit. The name is preserved in several gold-mining districts and is sometimes spelled Arrastra.

Arrowhead. The places in San Bernardino County were named after the arrowhead-shaped mark on the mountainside, created after the final uplift of the San Bernardino Range.

Arroyo, a-roi'-oh. California has more than 150 streams and gulches which include in their names this word, which means 'watercourse.'

Artois, ar-tois [Glenn]. The place named Germantown in 1876 was given the French name Artois in 1918.

Asilomar, a-see'-lo-mar [Monterey]. The artificial name, coined from the Spanish *asilo* (refuge) and *mar* (sea), was given by the National Board of the Y.W.C.A. in 1913.

Atascadero, a-tas-ka-dehr'-oh. This pleasant-sounding word, found in several geographical names, means 'miry place.'

Atherton [San Mateo]. The town was built in the 1860's on the land of Faxon D. Atherton, father-in-law of Gertrude Atherton, novelist.

Auburn [Placer]. Members of the New York Volunteers who came to the rich mines named the settlement after Auburn, N.Y., in August, 1849.

Avalon [Santa Catalina Island]. The name of King Arthur's legendary Elysium was bestowed upon the town in 1887.

Avawatz Mountains [San Bernardino]. A Southern Piute Indian name, Ivawatch, was recorded for the mountains in 1891. Its original meaning was probably 'white sheep.' The present spelling was used by the Geological Survey in 1933.

Avenal, av'-e-nal [Kings]. The post office was established in 1930 and named after Avenal (oatfield) Creek.

Avila, a'-vi-la [San Luis Obispo]. Preserves the name of Miguel Avila, grantee in 1839 of Rancho San Miguelito, on which the town is situated.

Azusa [Los Angeles]. Named in 1887 after Rancho Azusa, on which it was built. The grant derived its name from the Indian village *asuksa-gna.*

Bakersfield [Kern]. Colonel Thomas Baker, who tried to develop a waterway from Kern Lake to San Francisco Bay in the early 1860's, had a corral here known as "Baker's field." In 1868 the name was transferred to the city.

Balboa [Orange]. Named in 1905 in honor of Vasco Núñez de Balboa, discoverer of the Pacific Ocean in 1513.

Baldwin Park [Los Angeles]. Named in 1912 for E. J. ("Lucky") Baldwin, a spectacular financier in the 'nineties, on whose former estate the city was built. Baldwin Lake [San Bernardino] was also named for him.

Bally, Bolly, Bully. The name, applied to mountains and hills in Shasta, Trinity, and Tehama counties, is derived from Wintun Indian *bola* (spirit) or *buli* (peak)—probably the same stem. Indians, like other primitive peoples, identified spirits with mountains. This is one of the few generic geographical terms of Indian origin in California.

Banning [Riverside]. Named in 1885 for Phineas Banning, of Delaware, after 1851 one of the outstanding pioneers in the development of the Los Angeles district.

Barstow [San Bernardino]. Named in 1886 by the Santa Fe R.R. for its president, William Barstow Strong.

Batequitos Lagoon, bah-tay-kee'-tohs [San Diego]. Padre Font in 1776 mentioned a place called "Los Batequitos, a small watering place" (from *batéqui*, 'a well dug in the sand').

Bear. Over five hundred features, among them seven rivers, are named for the largest of California's native animals.

Beckwourth Pass [Plumas]. For James P. Beckwourth, adventurer and guide, who discovered the emigrant route in 1851.

Beegum Peak [Tehama]. A Southern term for beehive, applied because of the shape of the peak as well as the presence of bee colonies in the holes of the limestone.

Bell [Los Angeles]. Named in 1910 by the founders of the town, A. and J. G. Bell.

Bellflower [Los Angeles]. Named in 1909 after an orchard of bellflower apples.

Belmont [San Mateo]. The place, settled in the 1850's, became the county seat in 1856. Belmont, a variant of Beaumont ('beautiful mountain' in French), is an international name.

Belvedere [Marin]. This popular place name of Italian origin, usually spelled Belvidere in the United States, was applied in 1890. A subdivision east of Los Angeles bore the name until it became a part of the metropolis.

Benicia, be-nee′-sha [Solano]. Founded in 1847 as a rival of Yerba Buena and named Francisca, one of the given names of M. G. Vallejo's wife. Changed to Benicia, another of her given names, when Yerba Buena became San Francisco.

Benson Lake [Yosemite N. P.]. Named in 1895 for Harry C. Benson, later acting superintendent of the Park.

Berkeley [Alameda]. In 1866 the new college town was named for the philosopher, Bishop George Berkeley, who wrote the famous line: "Westward the course of empire takes its way."

Berryessa Lake [Napa]. The name perpetuates the name of two brothers, grantees of Rancho Las Putas.

Beverly Hills [Los Angeles]. Named in 1907 by B. E. Green after Beverly Farms, Massachusetts.

Bidwell. Names in several counties commemorate John Bidwell, one of the great pioneers of northern California after 1841.

Bieber [Lassen]. The post office was named in 1879 for Nathan Bieber, who had built a store here in 1877.

Big Oak Flat Road [Tuolumne, Mariposa]. This road into Yosemite was named after the village Big Oak Flat, so named because a valley oak was uprooted there by miners.

Big Sur River [Monterey]. From the Spanish *Rio Grande del Sur* (big river of the south [of Monterey]).

Bishop [Inyo]. Named for Samuel A. Bishop, of Virginia, who came to California in 1849 and became a well-known cattleman. The name was first applied to the creek.

Blakes Sea [Riverside, Imperial]. The ancient lake bed, now partly filled by Salton Sea, commemorates W. P. Blake, geologist of the Railroad Survey, 1853.

Blythe [Riverside]. Named for Thomas H. Blythe, of San Francisco, a promoter of irrigation in the 1870's.

Bodega, bo-day'-ga [Sonoma]. The bay was entered by the Spanish ship *Sonora* on October 3, 1775, and was named for her captain, Juan Francisco de la Bodega y Quadra.

Bodie [Mono]. For Waterman S. Body (boh'dee), who discovered the mines in 1859 and died in a snowstorm in 1860.

Bohemotash Mountain [Shasta]. For an Indian campground near Shasta Dam. *Bohem* is the Wintun Indian word for 'large.'

Bolinas, bo-lee'-nas [Marin]. "La Cañada que llaman los Baulenes" (the valley that they call the Baulenes) was mentioned as early as 1834. The name refers to the Indians who lived there, but its meaning is no longer determinable. The Coast Survey until about 1910 spelled the name Ballenas, wrongly assuming it to be from the Spanish word for whales, *ballenas.*

Bollibokka Mountain [Shasta]. The name is derived from Wintun *bolla,* said to mean 'black,' and *bokka,* 'bush,' referring here to the black-berried manzanita.

Bolsa. The word, meaning 'pocket,' is found in many places along the coast. In a geographical sense it designates a place enclosed on three sides, accessible by a single route.

Bonita, Point [Marin]. The term *Punta Bonete* was used in 1794, because the original three hills at this point resembled the bonnets of clergymen. In later years the name was changed to the present spelling, which literally means 'pretty point.'

Borego [San Diego]. The Spanish word for lamb or sheep was frequently used for place names in Spanish times. The feminine form *borrega* was used more often than the masculine form, properly spelled *borrego.*

Bouquet Canyon [Los Angeles]. The canyon was known as *El Buque* (the ship), Spanish nickname of a French sailor who settled there, and American surveyors in the 1850's took this name for the French word *bouquet.*

Branciforte Creek, bran'-si-fort [Santa Cruz]. The creek takes the name from the *Pueblo de Branciforte,* established at the site of present Santa Cruz in 1797 and named in honor of the viceroy of New Spain, the Marquis of Branciforte.

Brawley [Imperial]. The town was laid out in 1902 and named for J. H. Braly, of Los Angeles. When Braly objected to the use of his name the present name was substituted.

Brea, bray'-a [Orange]. From a rancho called *Cañada de la Brea* (valley of pitch, or bitumen). In Los Angeles County the word *brea* occurs in the name of the pits—La Brea—in which are preserved the skeletons of thousands of extinct animals. The word appeared in the names of five land grants and is also preserved in Labrea Creek [Santa Barbara].

Brewer, Mount [Tulare]. Named in 1864 for William H. Brewer, first assistant in the Whitney Survey, 1860–1864.

Breyfogle [Death Valley]. Two places here commemorate Charles Breyfogle, who in 1864 discovered the "lost mine."

Brisbane [San Mateo]. Named in 1908 for Arthur Brisbane, a well-known journalist, who built one of the first houses.

Broderick, Mount [Yosemite N. P.]. Named in memory of U. S. Senator David C. Broderick, who was killed in the last formal duel fought on California soil (1859).

Buchon, bu-shon', Point [San Luis Obispo]. Named after an Indian village; in 1769 soldiers of the Portolá expedition called the chief (and hence the village) El Buchon because he had an enormous goiter (Span., *buchón*).

Buena Park [Orange] A half-Spanish name (*buena,* 'good'), given to the town in 1887 and the Santa Fe station in 1929.

Buena Vista, bway-na vis-ta. The California places were apparently all named because they command a 'beautiful view,' not to commemorate Taylor's victory at Buena Vista.

Bully Choop [Shasta, Trinity]. The name is derived from the Wintun Indian *buli chup* (sharp peak). Recorded by the Whitney Survey in the 1860's as Bullet Chup. *See* Bally.

Bumpass Hell or **Hot Springs** [Lassen N. P.]. Named for Kendall V. Bumpass, a hunter and prospector of the 1860's and for the boiling mud pots and steam vents.

Bunker Hill. At least six hills and peaks were named after the famous battleground in Boston.

Bunnell Point [Yosemite N. P.]. Named for Lafayette H. Bunnell, who was with the first party of white men known to have entered Yosemite Valley, March 25, 1851.

Burbank [Los Angeles]. Named for Dr. David Burbank, a Los Angeles dentist, in 1887.

Burbank Memorial Park [Sonoma]. The home and experimental garden of Luther Burbank (1849–1926), famous horticulturist.

Buriburi Ridge [San Mateo]. A place called Buriburi was mentioned as early as 1798, and applied to a land grant in 1827. The name is Indian but its meaning is not known.

Burlingame [San Mateo]. Named in 1868 for Anson Burlingame, orator and diplomat, U. S. Minister to China from 1861 to 1867.

Butano [San Mateo]. The name has been mentioned since 1816. It refers to a drinking horn or a spring suggesting one.

Butte. The geographical term was introduced into western America by French Canadian trappers, who used it for an isolated peak.

Cabazon, kab'-a-zone [Riverside]. The station was named in the 1870's, after a rancheria near by, so named because the chief had an unusually large head (*cabezón*).

Cabrillo, ka-bree'-oh, ka-bril'-loh. The national monument in San Diego and the points in Monterey and Mendocino counties honor Juan Rodríguez Cabrillo, the Portuguese navigator in Spanish service, who, in 1542, was the first to sail up the coast of what is now the state of California.

Cache Creek, kash [Yolo]. So named before 1832 by the Hudson's Bay trappers who cached furs and supplies near by.

Cahuenga Pass, ka-weng'-ga, ka-hung'-ga [Los Angeles]. The pass derived its name from the Cahuenga Rancho, which was named after an Indian rancheria mentioned as *Caguenga* as early as 1802. At "Campo de Cahuenga" General Andrés Pico surrendered to Frémont, January 13, 1847.

Cahuilla [Riverside]. *See* Coachella.

Cajon Pass, ka-hohn' [San Bernardino]. The word means 'box' in Spanish and as a geographical term was used to describe boxlike canyons. The canyon which gave the name to the pass on the old Spanish trail was mentioned in 1806 as "el cajon que llaman Muscupiavit" (the canyon called Muscupiavit), a name which was probably given because of the Indian village of Muscupiavit near by.

Cal-. The first syllable of California is found in a number of coined border names. Calada, Calvada, Calneva are found along the Nevada line; Calor connects with Oregon (Caldor in El Dorado County, however, stands for California Door Company), Calzona with Arizona, Calexico with Mexico.

Calabazas, kal-a-bass'-as. The Spanish word for pumpkins, squash, or gourds has been preserved in Los Angeles (here spelled Calabasas), Santa Clara, and Sonoma counties.

Calaveras, kal-a-vehr'-as. The name, meaning 'skulls,' was repeatedly used in Spanish times for places where human skeletons testified to a fight or a famine. The place from which the names for creek, valley, and dam in Santa Clara and Alameda counties are derived was mentioned as early as 1809. The name applied to Calaveras river, county, and state park originated when John Marsh and his party found a great many skulls and skeletons near the river in 1836 or 1837.

Calexico [Imperial]. Coined in 1901 from *Cali*fornia and *Me*xico. The settlement on the Mexican side is Mexicali.

Calico Hills [San Bernardino], **Calico Peaks** [Death Valley]. A term used by prospectors in the desert region for volcanic rocks with colors varying from yellowish to buff and from pinkish to red.

Caliente, kal-i-en'-te. The word means 'hot' in Spanish. The canyon in Kern County and the range in San Luis Obispo County, however, were not named because of the climate, but after near-by hot springs.

California. California, like El Dorado, Quivira, and The Seven Cities of Cibola, was the name of one of the utopias which originated in the imagination of the people after the discovery of America had revived the age-old dream of a paradise on earth. The mythical realm was apparently created by the Spanish writer Montalvo in the romance *Las Sergas de Esplandián* (the exploits of Esplandian) and endowed with beautiful black Amazons, gold, and pearls.

The name is a fanciful creation; none of the many explanations of the meaning of California can be substantiated. *Golfo de la California* and a *Cabo California* appear on maps of 1562. In 1569 the name was applied to the peninsula of what is now Lower California; on later maps it was often extended to include the entire Pacific coast. From 1769 to 1846 the area which is approximately included in the present state was termed *Alta* (upper), or *Nueva* (new), California.

Calipatria [Imperial]. The name was coined from *Cali*fornia and *patria* (Latin, 'fatherland') and was applied to the place in 1914.

Calistoga [Napa]. Sam Brannan, who developed the place as a resort in 1859, is said to have declared that he would make his place the Saratoga of California, but his tongue twisted and he said he would make it the Calistoga of Sarifornia.

Calpella [Mendocino]. The name of a chief of a Pomo Indian village mentioned in 1851; also applied to the village, and then to all the Indians of Redwood Valley.

Calpine [Sierra]. Known as McAlpine in 1919. When the post office was established the abbreviated form was used.

Camanche [Calaveras]. Named in 1849 by a miner, after his home town in Iowa, which preserves the name of the great Indian tribe now spelled Comanche.

Cambria [San Luis Òbispo]. The place was settled in the 1860's and given the Roman name of ancient Wales.

Camino, ka-mee'-noh. The Spanish word for 'road' is repeatedly found in California place names. El Camino Real (the public highway) is the modern highway along the route which connected the various missions along the coast. It is often erroneously interpreted to mean 'the king's highway.'

Camp Curry [Yosemite N. P.]. Established and named in 1899 by David and Jennie Curry.

Camp Meeker [Sonoma]. Named for Melvin C. Meeker, early lumberman.

Campo. The word means 'field' in Spanish but in California is usually used in the sense of 'camp.'

Camulos [Ventura]. The name of an Indian village mentioned in 1804, recorded in a land grant in 1843, and applied to the Southern Pacific station in the 1870's.

Cañada. The Spanish word for valley, unlike the terms canyon and arroyo, has not entered our language. In a few places the name has survived from Spanish times, and American surveyors have used the term for gulches and valleys in Ventura and Santa Barbara counties. On the topographical maps of the War Department the Spanish spelling, cañada, has been restored. The pronunciation varies in different parts of the state: ca'-na-da, ca-na'-da, can-yah'-da.

Canby [Modoc]. The post office was named in 1880 for General E. R. S. Canby, killed by Indians in the Modoc War of 1873.

Capay, kay-pay' [Yolo]. An Indian word for 'stream' repeatedly found in Winṯun Indian territory (western drainage of the Sacramento). The names of the town and valley in Yolo County come from the Indian village, *Capa* (1821), *Copeh* (1851). *Cañada de Capay* was a land grant of 1846.

Capitola, kap-i-toh'-la [Santa Cruz]. The name was apparently coined from "capitol" when the place was developed as a resort by F. H. Hihn of Santa Cruz in 1876.

Carlsbad [San Diego]. Named in 1886 after the famous German Karlsbad in Bohemia because the mineral waters found in the two places are similar in composition.

Carmel, kar-mel' [Monterey]. The river was discovered by Vizcaíno, January 3, 1603, and called *Rio del Carmelo*, probably because three friars of the Carmelite order were with the expedition. The bay was also named in Spanish times; Mount Carmel was named by the Coast Survey in 1856; the modern Carmel-by-the-Sea was so called to distinguish it from another Carmel which was some ten miles inland. The Spanish spelling was used until the 1860's.

Carpinteria, kar-pin-te-ree'-a [Santa Barbara]. "The Indians have many canoes, and at the time were building one, for which reason the soldiers [of the Portolá expedition] named this village La Carpintería" (Crespi, Aug. 17, 1769). The name, meaning 'carpenter shop,' was preserved when it was applied to the post office in 1868.

Carquinez, kar-kee'-nes [Solano, Contra Costa]. The name of the Indians living at the strait has been used since 1795. Its meaning is 'traders.'

Carrizo Creek, kah-ree'-soh [San Diego, Imperial]. The presence of *carrizo* (reed grass), which later gave the name to the stream, was mentioned by Font when the Anza party camped here, December 13, 1775.

Carson River, Pass [Alpine]. Frémont named the river for "Kit" Carson, who guided him across the Sierra in 1844.

Casa. The place names which contain the Spanish word for house were probably all applied in American times. **Casa Blanca** [Riverside] was so named by the Santa Fe in 1887 because a white house could be seen from the station.

Cascade Range. The south part of the range extends into California to the gap south of Lassen Peak. The Cascades of Columbia River gave the name to the mountains.

Casmalia [Santa Barbara]. Probably a Spanish rendering of an Indian word, the meaning of which is now unknown, recorded as Casmali in 1837.

Caspar [Mendocino]. Named for Siegfrid Caspar, who settled here in the 1860's.

Castaic, kas-tayk' [Los Angeles, Kern]. The Chumash Indians apparently called the village at the foot of a trail over the mountains *Kashtik* ('my eyes' or 'our eye'), used here perhaps in the sense of 'view.' The name of the lake and the valley in Kern County was spelled Castac.

Castro. A number of place names commemorate the names of the various Castro families, some of whom played important roles in Spanish and Mexican times.

Cayucos, kah-yoo'-kas [San Luis Obispo]. The word appears in the secondary name of a land grant of 1837 and 1842, *Morro y Cayucos*. The name is probably derived from *cayuco* (fishing canoe), apparently a Spanish rendering of the Eskimo *kayak*. Font described a *cayuco* in 1776.

Cazadero, kaz-a-deh'-roh [Sonoma]. The name, meaning 'hunting place' in California Spanish, was applied to the terminal of the North Pacific Coast R.R. in the late 1880's.

Central Valley [Shasta]. When construction was begun in 1938 on Shasta Dam, main unit of the Central Valley Project, the two towns which developed were simply called Central Valley and Project City.

Ceres [Stanislaus]. The name of the Roman goddess of growing vegetation was given to the station shortly after this part of the Central Pacific was built in 1870–1871.

Cerrito, ser-ree'-toh. The word, meaning 'small hill,' was a favorite geographical term in Spanish California and has survived in several places.

Cerro. The Spanish generic term for peak or hill is still used in the southern part of the state for peak: Cerro Alto, Cerro Gordo, Cerro San Luis Obispo, etc.

Chagoopah [Tulare]. The falls and plateau were named in 1881 for an old Piute chief by that name.

Chalone [San Benito, Monterey]. An Indian tribe which lived east of Soledad Mission. The name is mentioned in 1816; a *Cierro Chalon* is on a map of the San Lorenzo land grant.

Chamise, Chamisal. *Chamiso* was the Chumash Indian name for the islay, or holly-leaved cherry; in Spanish and early American times the term chamisal was loosely used for a dense growth of brush, like chaparral; now botanists associate the name with our native white-flowering greasewood. As a place name it is found in Monterey, Colusa, San Benito, Mendocino, and other counties.

Chaparral, shap-a-ral'. The original Spanish word meant a thick growth of scrub oak. In California the name applies to dense, sometimes impenetrable, thickets of shrubs covering hillsides, and appears in many geographical terms.

Chemehuevi, shem-e-hway'-vi [San Bernardino]. The Indian tribe which gave its name to the valley and mountains is often mentioned (with various spellings) in Spanish and early American times.

Cherokee. Five camps were named for members of the Eastern Indian tribe who mined there in early gold-rush days. A town in Butte County, a settlement in San Joaquin County, and several minor features preserve the name.

Chico, chee′-koh [Butte]. The origin of the name is found in the land grant *Arroyo Chico* (little stream) of 1844. In 1849 John Bidwell acquired the land and laid out the town. The original arroyo is now called Big Chico Creek (big little creek), and the stream to the south Little Chico Creek (little little creek).

Chiles [Napa]. Named for Joseph B. Chiles, pioneer of 1841, who settled here in 1844.

China, Chinese. One of the most common place names derived from a nationality. It bears witness to the important part Chinese labor played in the building of the state. Some places, such as Chinese (locally: Chinee) Camp, go back to early mining days.

Chino [San Bernardino]. In Mexico and other Spanish-speaking countries the term designates a person of mixed blood. The chief of the original village on the *Santa Ana del Chino* grant, 1841, was probably a *chino.*

Chinquapin [Yosemite N. P.]. The Indian name for the native shrub, which grows here in abundance.

Chiquito, chi-kee′-toh [Madera]. The name goes back to the *Joaquin Chiquito* (little Joaquin [River]), probably applied by Mexican miners.

Chittenden [Yosemite N. P.]. The peak was named for Captain Hiram M. Chittenden, boundary commissioner for Yosemite National Park in 1904.

Cholame, sho-lam′ [San Luis Obispo]. The name of a Salinan Indian rancheria, mentioned as *Cholan* in 1803, and applied to the Cholam land grant in 1844.

Chollas, choll′-as [San Diego]. A *rancheria de las Choyas* is mentioned in 1775. The name probably comes from the name of the well-known cholla cactus, native of the region.

Chowchilla [Madera, Mariposa]. The *Chauciles* Indians are mentioned repeatedly in the 1830's as horse thieves. The name was applied to the river in the 1850's.

Chual [Santa Clara]. The name of the peak contains the Costanoan Indian word for pigweed or lamb's quarters, *chual,* valuable as a food. **Chualar,** choo′-a-lar [Monterey] means 'place where *chual* grows.' In 1830 the place was one of the landmarks delineating the jurisdiction of Monterey; in 1831 and 1835 the name was applied to land grants.

Chuckawalla. There are several places in the southeast corner of the state named for the large desert lizard.

Chula Vista [San Diego]. Named in 1880 from *chula,* Mexican for 'pretty,' 'graceful,' and the Spanish word for 'view.'

Chupines Creek, choo-pee'-nes [Monterey]. A place named Chupines was recorded in 1828 and an *Arroyo de los Chopines* in 1834. Probably from the Mexican *chopo* (black cottonwood), a native tree of the region.

Cienega, see-en'-e-ga. The Spanish word for marsh, often used to designate 'meadow' in America, was formerly a common place name, but has survived only for a few creeks.

Cima, see'-ma [San Bernardino]. The Spanish word for summit was applied to the station in 1907.

Cisco [Placer]. Named in 1865 by the Central Pacific R. R., for John J. Cisco, treasurer of the company, 1863–1869.

Clair Engle Lake [Trinity]. The large artificial lake created by Trinity Dam in 1965 was named in honor of Clair Engle, 1911-1964, U. S. Senator from California.

Claremont [Los Angeles]. Named in 1887 for Claremont, New Hampshire, home of a director of the development company.

Clarence King, Mount [Kings Canyon N. P.]. Named by the Whitney Survey in 1864 for one of its members, who became first director of the U. S. Geological Survey in 1879.

Clark, Mount [Yosemite N. P.]. Named for Galen Clark, first guardian of Yosemite when it was made a state park in 1864.

Cleveland National Forest. Created and named July 1, 1908, for President Cleveland, who had died a week before.

Clovis [Fresno]. Named for Clovis Cole, through whose land the Southern Pacific built a branch line in 1889.

Coachella [Riverside]. The valley north of Salton Sea was named for the Cahuilla Indians, whose name is preserved south of San Bernardino National Forest. When the region north of Salton Sea was surveyed before 1900, the name Conchilla Valley was suggested but disregarded, and the present meaningless name was substituted and made official in 1909.

Coalinga, koh-ling'-ga [Fresno]. The place was known as Coaling Station in 1888. A Southern Pacific official created the new name by adding an *a* to "coaling."

Coches Canyon, koh'-ches [San Diego]. The name, 'hog canyon,' is derived from the name of the land grant, *Cañada de los Coches,* of 1843. The Mexican provincial word *coche,* for 'hog,' was applied elsewhere in Spanish California.

Cocopah [Imperial]. An Indian tribe of the Yuman family, first mentioned in 1775 as *Cucapa.*

Cojo, koh'-hoh. The word, meaning 'lame,' or 'lame man,' was a favorite nickname in Spanish times and was often used in place names; at least one has survived: **Cañada del Cojo** [Santa Barbara], applied by the Portolá expedition in 1769 to a rancheria whose chief was lame.

Colby. The name of the mountain in Yosemite and the names of the pass and lake in Kings Canyon National Park honor William E. Colby, well-known conservationist and mountaineer.

Colfax [Placer]. Named in 1865 by the Central Pacific, for Schuyler Colfax, at that time Speaker of the House, later Vice-President with Grant.

Collayomi Valley, kal'-i-oh'-mee [Lake]. Probably a division of the Wappo Indians dwelling on both sides of the St. Helena range. A rancheria, *Cuaguillomic,* is mentioned in 1821; the name appears in titles of several land grants.

Colma [San Mateo]. On early maps the place is simply designated as Schoolhouse Station. The present name is mentioned in a directory of 1872; it may be a transfer name from Switzerland, where Colma is found as a place name.

Coloma [El Dorado]. Developed around Sutter's mill after the discovery of gold in January, 1848. It was named after a Maidu Indian village and was recorded as *Culloma* in the *New Helvetia Diary,* March 17, 1848.

Colony [Tulare]. The name for mills, meadow, and peak is all that remains of the Kaweah Co-operative Colony, organized in 1886 to market lumber on a socialistic basis.

Colorado River. The name was applied in 1604 to the present Little Colorado in Arizona "because the water is nearly red." In 1700 the name was identified with the great river. American cartographers tried to substitute Red River.

Colton [San Bernardino]. The station was named in 1875 for David D. Colton, financial director of the Central Pacific.

Colusa, ko-loo'-sa. The name of a rancheria, *Coru,* mentioned in 1821, is the source of this name, as well as of those of two land grants, *Coluses* (1844) and *Colus* (1845). From a variety of spellings Colusi emerged as the name of the county in 1850; in 1854 the present spelling was used.

Comptche, kompt'-she [Mendocino]. The name is probably derived from that of a Pomo Indian village.

Compton [Los Angeles]. The town was laid out by Griffith D. Compton in 1869.

Conception, Point [Santa Barbara]. The name *Punta de la Limpia Concepcion* was applied to the cape by Vizcaíno in 1602, because he reached it on December 8, the day of the *Purisima Concepción* (Immaculate Conception). The nearby post office is spelled the Spanish but pronounced the American way.

Concord [Contra Costa]. The settlement was founded in 1862 by Salvio Pacheco and named Todos Santos. A strong New England element changed the name (before 1873) to Concord, after the historic town in Massachusetts.

Concow [Butte]. The name of a branch of the Maidu Indians, derived from *Ko-yoan-kau* (place of the plains).

Conejo, ko-nay'-o [Ventura]. The Spanish name for rabbit, found repeatedly in place names of Spanish California, was used by Font for this place in 1776 and was applied to a land grant in 1822.

Conness, Mount [Yosemite N. P.]. Named by the Whitney Survey in 1864, for John Conness, U. S. senator, 1863–1869, who introduced the bill granting Yosemite Valley and the Mariposa Grove to the state of California.

Contra Costa. The county was created and named in 1850. The term, designating the 'coast opposite' San Francisco, had long been in use.

Converse [Fresno]. Named for Charles Converse, who took up timber lands in the valley in the 1870's. He built the first jail in the county and was first to be confined in it.

Convict Lake [Mono]. On September 24, 1871, a posse here fought with convicts escaped from Carson City, Nevada.

Copco Lake [Siskiyou]. Coined from *C*alifornia-*O*regon *P*ower *Co*mpany and applied about 1915.

Corning [Tehama]. Named in 1882 in memory of John Corning, official of the Central Pacific, who died in 1878.

Corona [Riverside]. The Latin word for circle was applied in 1896 because of the circular drive around the city; this was the scene of spectacular auto races, 1913–1916.

Coronado [San Diego]. Named in 1887 after the islands off the coast of Lower California, *Los Coronados,* which in turn had been named by Vizcaíno in 1602.

Corral, kor-ral'. In western states the Spanish word for enclosed space or poultry yard means 'pen for livestock'; it is found in many California place names.

Corralitos [Santa Cruz]. The name, 'little corrals,' was mentioned in 1807 and was applied to a land grant in 1823.

Corte Madera [Marin]. The origin of the name, which means 'place where lumber or timber is cut,' is found in the *Corte de Madera del Presidio* land grant of 1834. The name is also found in other sections of the state.

Coso [Inyo]. *Coso* apparently means 'fire' in the Shoshonean Indian dialect of the region referred to as 'burnt district.' Used in a geographical sense since 1860.

Costa Mesa [Orange]. The post office was established and named in 1921. The name is an Americanized combination of two Spanish words, *costa* (coast) and *mesa* (tableland), chosen as a result of a contest.

Cosumnes River, ko-sum'-nes [Sacramento]. A *rancheria de los Cossomnes,* or *Cossmines,* and a tribe, *Cosemenes,* were recorded in the 1820's. The present spelling was used by Sutter in 1841 and in two land grants of 1844. The ending *-umne* means 'people'; the root may mean 'salmon.'

Cotati [Sonoma]. The name of an Indian rancheria, *Kotati,* was applied in the present form to a land grant in 1844.

Coutolenc, koht'-o-links [Butte]. For Eugene Coutolanezes; abbreviated when the post office was opened in the 1880's.

Covelo, koh'-ve-loh [Mendocino]. Named in 1870, probably not after a fortress in Switzerland, as the story goes, but after Covolo, the old Venetian fort in adjoining Tirol.

Covina, ko-vee'-nah [Los Angeles]. The euphonious but apparently meaningless name was applied to the town in the 1880's.

Coyote, ky-oh'-tee, ky'-oht. A western American adaptation of the Mexican name for the prairie wolf, *coyotl*, and an extremely popular place name, especially in California. The names in the mining districts are often derived from "coyoteing," i.e., mining in irregular shafts or burrows, comparable to the holes of coyotes.

Crescent City [Del Norte]. Named in the early 1850's for the crescent-shaped bay. There are many other features so named and a fanciful La Crescenta in Los Angeles County.

Crockett [Contra Costa]. Named in 1867 for Judge J. B. Crockett, of the California Supreme Court.

Crows Landing [Stanislaus]. The name commemorates Walter J. Crow, who settled here after 1849.

Cucamonga [San Bernardino]. A Shoshonean Indian place name, mentioned in 1819 and transferred to a land grant in 1839. The meaning is 'sandy place.'

Cuesta Pass, kwest'-a [San Luis Obispo]. The name (Spanish, 'grade') was applied to a station north of the pass when construction engineers of the Southern Pacific achieved the difficult task of crossing the Santa Lucia Range, 1887–1894. The pass had been called *Cañada de la Cuesta* in 1842.

Culver City [Los Angeles]. Named for Harry H. Culver, who subdivided part of the Ballona land grant in 1914.

Cupertino, kew-per-tee'-no, koo-per-tee'-no [Santa Clara]. The *Arroyo de San Jose Cupertino,* named in honor of an Italian saint of the 17th century, was mentioned by Anza and Font in 1776. The arroyo is now Stevens Creek, but the post office preserves the old name.

Cuyama River [Ventura, San Luis Obispo, Santa Barbara]. The name is derived from a Chumash Indian place name,

Kuyam, meaning 'clams.' An *arroyo llamado de Cuyam* (a creek called of Cuyam), recorded in 1824, probably was the river. The present version is repeatedly found in land-grant papers. The pronunciation varies according to locality: kwee-ah'-ma, kwee-yam'-a, koo-yah'-ma.

Cuyamaca, kwee-a-mah'-ka [San Diego]. A rancheria, spelled *Cullamac* and *Cuyamac,* is mentioned in mission records after 1776. In 1845 the present spelling was used for a land grant and for the mountains. The designation "Queermack," commonly used for the mountains, seems to indicate that the Diegueño Indian *ekwi-amak* (rain above) may be connected with the name.

Daly City [San Mateo]. The city came into existence when people found a refuge here after the San Francisco fire of 1906, and was named for John Daly, who had been a dairyman of the district since the 1850's.

Dana, Mount [Yosemite N. P.]. Named by the Whitney Survey in 1863, for James D. Dana, American geologist.

Dana, Point [Orange]. Named in 1884 by the Coast Survey, for Richard H. Dana, author of *Two Years Before the Mast.*

Dantes View [Death Valley]. The name, probably inspired by Dante's description of the Inferno, was applied to the viewpoint in the early 1930's; however, Dante Springs near Soda Lake was mentioned much earlier.

Dardanelles. The mountains were so named by the Whitney Survey, apparently because their peaks resemble the castles guarding the entrance to the straits in Turkey.

Darwin, Mount [Fresno]. Named in 1895 for Charles Darwin, father of the theory of evolution. *See* Evolution.

Darwin Canyon [Inyo]. Named in 1860 when Darwin French searched here for the mythical "Gunsight lode."

Davidson, Mount [San Francisco]. Named in 1912 for George Davidson, the geographer, who had died in 1911.

Davis [Yolo]. Named for Jerome C. Davis, who settled here in the early 1850's.

Death Valley. The name, recorded since 1861, was probably applied by prospectors because of the forbidding appearance of the valley and of the presence of skeletons of travelers who died from heat or thirst.

Delano, de-lay'-noh [Kern]. Named by the Southern Pacific in 1873 for Columbus Delano, then Secretary of the Interior.

Delgada, Point [Humboldt]. The name, meaning 'narrow,' was applied to Point Arena by Bodega in 1775, and transferred in 1841 to the present point, which is not at all narrow.

Del Mar [San Diego]. The name was suggested in 1885 by Bayard Taylor's poem "The Fight of Paso del Mar."

Del Monte, del mon'-tee [Monterey]. The name, meaning 'of the grove,' was first applied to the hotel in 1886, suggested probably by the beautiful oak groves near by.

Del Norte. The Spanish phrase 'of the north' was bestowed upon the new county by the legislature in 1857.

Del Rey [Fresno]. Named in 1898 after the Rio del Rey (river of the king) Ranch, on which the new railroad station was built. *See* Kings River.

Descanso, des-kan'-soh [San Diego]. The name, meaning 'repose' in Spanish, was applied to the post office in the 1880's. A place named Descanso, across the border in Lower California, was recorded in 1845.

Devil. In spite of the many holy names in the state, the Prince of Darkness has succeeded in connecting his name with almost 200 topographical features, including Devils Speedway and Golf Course [Death Valley], Devils Parade Ground [Tehama], Devils Rock Garden [Shasta], Devils Bath Tub [Fresno], Devils Pulpit [Mount Diablo State Park], Devils Postpile National Monument.

Diablo, dee-ah'-bloh, dy-ab'-loh, **Mount** [Contra Costa]. The name *Monte del Diablo* (devil's grove) for an Indian rancheria was recorded about 1824. It is reported that a fight between Spanish soldiers and Indians took place by a thicket near the site of what is now Pacheco, and that a grotesquely dressed Indian medicine man made the soldiers believe the devil had allied himself with the Indians. American explorers, believing that *monte* meant 'mountain' as in Italian, transferred the name to the peak.

Dinkey Creek [Fresno]. Named in August, 1863, by four hunters whose dog Dinkey was injured fighting a grizzly.

Dinuba, dy-noo´-ba [Tulare]. Probably a fanciful creation of the construction engineer of the Southern Pacific who in 1887 chose such names as Fortuna and Taurusa for stations along this line.

Disaster Peak [Alpine]. On September 6, 1877, W. A. Cowles, a topographer of the Wheeler Survey, accidentally dislodged a huge boulder on the peak and was severely injured.

Donner Lake, Pass, Peak [Nevada, Placer]. In the winter of 1846–47, eighty-one immigrants led by George and Jacob Donner had to winter near the lake; almost half of them died of cold and starvation, some resorting to cannibalism.

Don Pedro Reservoir [Tuolumne]. Named after Don Pedro's Bar, in turn named for Pierre (Don Pedro) Sainsevain, French pioneer of 1839, who mined here in 1848.

Dos Palos [Merced]. So named by the Southern Pacific in 1889. *Dos Pálos* (two trees) was mentioned in 1841.

Dos Rios [Mendocino]. Named 'two rivers' because of its position at the junction of two branches of the Eel River.

Downey [Los Angeles]. In 1865 John G. Downey, governor of California from 1860 to 1862, subdivided the Santa Gertrudis Rancho and gave his name to the new town.

Downieville [Sierra]. Named for William Downie, a Scot who mined gold at the forks of Yuba River in 1849.

Drakes Bay [Marin]. The name of the English navigator, Francis Drake, appeared after 1625 on maps for a bay in the general region. Since 1793 the name has been identified with the present bay although it has never been proved that this was where Drake anchored in 1579. *See* Albion.

Duarte, dwar´-tee [Los Angeles]. Named for Andrés Duarte, who settled on his Rancho Azusa in 1841.

Ducor [Tulare]. In 1899 the Southern Pacific station was given the abbreviated version of the former name, Dutch Corners, where the homesteads of four Germans joined.

Dumbarton [Alameda, San Mateo]. The name Dumbarton Point was applied to the station in 1876. Dumbarton is the name of a city in Scotland and of several towns in the East.

Dume, Point [Los Angeles]. The name was given to the cape by Vancouver in 1793, in honor of Padre Dumetz of Mission San Buenaventura, but was misspelled on Vancouver's map and has never been corrected.

Dunderberg Peak [Mono]. Named after the famous mine on Dog Creek, which had probably been named for the U. S. warship *Dunderberg,* which in turn had been named for Dunderberg (Dutch, 'thunder mountain'), New York.

Dunsmuir [Siskiyou]. The name was applied to the railroad station in 1886 for Alexander Dunsmuir, coal baron of British Columbia and San Francisco, who replied to the compliment by donating the fountain by the station.

Dutch. With the exception of the Yankees, the Germans seem to be the only settlers whose presence is recorded by their nickname. Not all the hundred-odd Dutch creeks, canyons, flats refer to Germans or Netherlanders.

Earlimart [Tulare]. An advertising name applied in 1909 to indicate that crops mature early here.

Ebbetts Pass [Alpine]. Named in 1854 for John Ebbetts, who had crossed the pass with a mule train in April, 1851.

Edwards [Kern]. The airfield was named in 1950 for Capt. Glenn W. Edwards, killed in an experimental flight.

Eel River [Mendocino, Humboldt]. Named in January, 1850, by the Gregg exploring party, who obtained quantities of eels from the Indians in exchange for a broken frying pan.

El Cajon, ka-hohn' [San Diego]. The name means 'box' in Spanish and was applied in Spanish America for canyons boxed in by hills or cliffs. Mentioned as early as 1821 as the name of a rancho of Mission San Diego.

El Capitan, cap-i-tan' [Yosemite N. P.]. Named in 1851 by the Mariposa Battalion, discoverers of the valley, who assumed that *El Capitan* (the captain, or chief) was the Spanish translation of the Indian name for the rock.

El Centro [Imperial]. Given the Spanish name in 1905 because of its position near the center of Imperial Valley.

El Cerrito, ser-ree'-toh [Contra Costa]. The name, 'small hill,' for the isolated knoll at the bay shore, was recorded in 1830 as *Serrito de San Antonio,* and in the 1850's as *Cerrito de San Pablo.* The present name was applied to the post office in 1912. *See* Cerrito.

El Dorado. The name, meaning 'the gilded one,' appeared at the beginning of the 16th century for a mythical Indian chief in South America who was covered with gold dust during the performance of ceremonies. Later the name simply designated one of the golden utopias and assumed new significance with the discovery of gold in California. The county was named in 1850.

Elk. The oldest of the many features named for the once common animal is probably Elk River, so called by the Gregg party on Christmas Day, 1849, after they had celebrated the day with a dinner of elk meat.

El Monte [Los Angeles]. The place was settled in the 1850's and called Monte (a grove or thicket) because of the dense growth of willows.

El Segundo [Los Angeles]. Applied by the Standard Oil Company in 1911 to its *second* refinery in California.

Elsinore [Riverside]. Named in 1884 after the Danish castle, made famous by Shakespeare's *Hamlet.*

Embarcadero, em-bar-ka-deh'-roh. The Spanish word for landing place has survived in a number of places.

Emerson, Mount [Inyo]. John Muir named a peak for the American poet and philosopher, Ralph Waldo Emerson, who visited Yosemite in 1871, and the name was later transferred to this peak.

Emeryville [Alameda]. Named for Joseph Emery, who in 1859 bought the land on which the city stands.

Encanto, en-kan'-toh [San Diego]. The Spanish word for 'enchantment' was applied to the post office in the 1890's.

Encinitas, en-si-nee'-tas [San Diego]. Settled in the 1880's and named after *Cañada de los Encinitos* (valley of the little oaks), recorded in 1839. *Encina* (live oak) and its diminutive, *encinita,* are frequent in California place names.

Escondido, es-kon-dee'-doh [San Diego]. The Spanish word for 'hidden' was applied to the subdivision in 1885. There are four Escondido Creeks in southern counties.

Espada Creek [San Diego]. On August 27, 1769, an Indian from a near-by village stole the sword of one of Portolá's soldiers, whereupon the place was named *Rancheria de la Espada* (village of the sword).

Estero, es-teh′-roh. The Spanish word for inlet or estuary is frequently found along the ocean shore.

Estrella, es-treh′-ya [San Luis Obispo]. The name 'star' was applied in Mexican times because four valleys diverge like the rays of a star at the original site of the ranch.

Etiwanda [San Bernardino]. Named in the early 1880's for the chief of an Indian tribe near Lake Michigan.

Ettawa [Lake]. Coined before 1900 by the owner of the springs from the name of his mother, Etta Waughtel.

Ettersburg [Humboldt]. The post office was named in 1904 for Albert F. Etter, creator of new fruit varieties.

Eureka [Humboldt]. The Greek expression 'I have found it' became popular when the Constitutional Convention in October, 1849, adopted it as the motto for the Great Seal of California. The city, named in May, 1850, is probably the oldest place in the United States bearing the name.

Evolution Group. The mountain peaks comprising the group were named by Theodore S. Solomons in July, 1895, in honor of Charles Darwin, Thomas Huxley, Herbert Spencer, Alfred Wallace (British), Ernst Haeckel (German), and John Fiske (American), who were at that time the leading exponents of the theory of evolution. Jean Lamarck (French) was added to the group in 1912, and Gregor Mendel (German-Austrian) in 1942.

Exeter [Tulare]. The name of the city in England was chosen for the community by English settlers.

Fairfax [Marin]. Charles ("Lord") Fairfax of Fairfax County, Virginia, settled here in 1856.

Fairfield [Solano]. Named in 1859 by Robert Waterman, clipper-ship captain, after his former home in Connecticut.

Fallen Leaf Lake [El Dorado]. Named before 1874, probably because of its appearance when viewed from near-by mountains.

Fall River [Shasta]. Named by Frémont in 1846 because of its falls and cascades.

Fandango [Modoc]. According to the most reliable source, an immigrant party gave the name to the valley in the fall of 1849 when cold weather forced them to dance all night to keep warm.

Farallon Islands [San Francisco]. The Spanish name for small rocky islands in the sea is shown on old maps of the coast. The rocks outside the Golden Gate were mentioned as *farallones* by the Vizcaíno expedition in 1603, and were named *Farallones de los Frayles* by Bodega in 1775.

Feather River. Sutter said that he named the river *Rio de las Plumas* (river of feathers) in the 1840's because of the many feathers worn by the Indians and the feathers scattered over the landscape. The name Feather River had been used by Hudson's Bay trappers in the 1830's, but it was upon Sutter's statement that it was put on the maps.

Felton [Santa Cruz]. Named in 1878 for Charles N. Felton, congressman (1885–1889) and U. S. senator (1891–1893).

Fermin, Point [Los Angeles]. Given to the point by Vancouver in 1793, in honor of Padre Fermín Francisco de Lasuén.

Fernandez Pass [Madera]. Named for Joseph Fernandez, member of a detachment of the U. S. Fourth Cavalry, which explored the headwaters of the Merced in 1896–1897.

Fiddletown [Amador]. The place, which was settled by miners from Missouri in 1849, received its name because many of them possessed and played fiddles. From 1876 to 1932 the name of the town was Oleta.

Fillmore [Ventura]. Named in 1887 for J. A. Fillmore, general superintendent of the Southern Pacific.

Firebaugh [Fresno]. In 1854 A. D. Fierbaugh established a trading post and ferry at this point. The name was misspelled when it was used for a stage station in the 1860's.

Flintridge [Los Angeles]. Named in 1920 for Frank P. Flint, U. S. senator, 1905–1911.

Folsom [Sacramento]. The town was laid out in 1855 by Theodore D. Judah as the terminus of the Sacramento Valley R.R., the first in California. Joseph L. Folsom was assistant quartermaster of the New York Volunteers in 1847, and later was owner of the rancho on which the place is situated.

Fontana [San Bernardino]. Named in 1913 for the Fontana Development Company. The name may be the Spanish poetical word for fountain or the name of a family.

Fort Bragg [Mendocino]. Named after the military post established in 1857 and named for Colonel Braxton Bragg, Mexican War veteran and afterward Confederate general.

Fort Jones [Siskiyou]. In 1860 the settlers named the town after the fort, in gratitude for the military protection they had received. The fort had been named in 1852 for Colonel Roger Jones, adjutant general of the army.

Fort Ross [Sonoma]. The Russian settlement in California was established on September 11, 1812, and the name was drawn by lot, the lots having been placed at the base of the image of Christ. *Ross* is an obsolete, poetical name for 'Russians.'

Fortuna [Humboldt]. The original name Fortune, applied in the 1870's, was changed to the present form because it sounded better and still had the same advertising value.

Fourth Crossing [Calaveras]. Named before 1855 because here the fourth fork of the Calaveras was forded.

Fredonyer Pass [Lassen]. Discovered by Atlas Fredonyer in 1852.

Fremont. One of the most spectacular characters in United States history, J. C. Frémont, is commemorated in the city in Alameda County, incorporated in 1956, and in two state parks, Fremont Fort [Merced] and Fremont Peak [San Benito], although the hill at the head of Steinbach Canyon, where Frémont raised the flag in 1846, is not in the Park.

French. Most of the seventy-five places so called were named for French Canadian trappers or French settlers.

Fresno. The name, Spanish for ash, was applied because the tree was native here. Fresno River [Madera] was mentioned in 1851, the county created in 1856, and the modern city founded in 1868 by the "German Syndicate" of which Frederick Roeding was one of the leaders.

Friant [Fresno]. In 1910 the Southern Pacific station of Pollasky was named for Thomas Friant, prominent lumberman. The dam was named after the town in 1939.

Fullerton [Orange]. Named in 1887 for G. H. Fullerton, president of the development company.

Funeral Mountains [Death Valley]. The name probably arose because the light-colored rock formations are capped with heavy masses of black limestone or basalt, the debris of which runs down the slopes, giving them the appearance of being fringed with mourning crepe.

Furnace Creek [Death Valley]. The name (which occurs elsewhere in the state) was applied by Dr. Darwin French in 1860, doubtless because of the extreme heat.

Gabilan Range [Monterey, San Benito]. Gabilan Peak was named for the sparrow hawk (Spanish, *gavilan*, or *gabilan*) and has been known by this name since 1828; it is popularly known as Fremont Peak.

Gallinas [Marin]. A *sitio de las Gallenas* (place of the hens) was mentioned in 1817.

Garberville [Humboldt]. The post office was named in 1874 for Jacob C. Garber, the first settler.

Garcia River [Mendocino]. Named for Rafael García, who had a land grant here in 1844.

Gardena [Los Angeles]. The name, doubtless coined from "garden," was applied to the subdivision in the 1880's.

Gardiner, Mount [Fresno]. Named in 1865 for James T. Gardiner, member of the Whitney Survey.

Gaviota [Santa Barbara]. The soldiers of the Portolá expedition on August 24, 1769, named the place where they camped *La Gaviota* because they had killed a sea gull there.

Gaylor Lakes [Yosemite N. P.]. Named in memory of Jack Gaylor, park ranger, who died in 1921.

Gazelle [Siskiyou]. The post office was named in 1874 for the African antelope, probably to distinguish it from the many places named for the native antelope.

Gerber [Tehama]. Post office and railroad station were named in 1916 for H. E. Gerber of Sacramento.

Gibbs, Mount [Yosemite N. P.]. Named in 1864 for Oliver W. Gibbs, professor of science at Harvard.

Gilroy [Santa Clara]. Named for John Gilroy, a Scotch sailor, who arrived in California in 1814, settled in the Santa Clara Valley, and in 1833 came into possession of the land on which the city is situated.

Glendale [Los Angeles]. The town was founded on the Rancho San Rafael about 1880 and named Riverdale. When the post office was established the name was changed because there was a Riverdale P.O. in Fresno County.

Glendora [Los Angeles]. Coined in 1887 by George Whitcomb from the word "glen" and his wife's name "Ledora."

Glenn County. The county was formed in 1891 and named for Dr. Hugh J. Glenn, pioneer of 1849 and for many years the leading wheat grower of California.

Goddard, Mount [Kings Canyon N. P.]. Named in 1864 by the Whitney Survey, for George H. Goddard, native of England and long a leading civil engineer in California.

Goethe, Mount [Fresno]. The highest peak of Glacier Divide was named in 1949, the bicentennial year of the birth of Johann Wolfgang Goethe, poet and philosopher.

Golden Gate. Named by Frémont in 1846 in analogy to the Golden Horn in Europe. He chose the name because he foresaw the day when riches of the Orient would flow through the gate, but he could not foresee that the discovery of gold in a few years would give the name new significance.

Goleta, go-lee'-ta [Santa Barbara]. The word means 'schooner' and was used as a name for a land grant in 1846. It is not certain whether the place was so named because of the wreck of an American schooner in the estuary or because a vessel was built here in 1829.

Gonzales [Monterey]. The railroad station was named in 1873 for Teodoro Gonzales because it was built on his extensive grant.

Gorda. The Spanish word for 'broad' or 'big' was used repeatedly for physical features. The point south of Cape Mendocino has retained the all-Spanish name, Punta Gorda.

Graciosa [Santa Barbara]. The name *La Graciosa* (the graceful one) was applied to a lagoon by soldiers of the Portolá
expedition on August 31, 1769. Seven years later Font said
it was so named because it was "small and of very fine
water." The ridge, *la cuesta de la graciosa,* is mentioned in
1824. The name was given to the station in 1880.

Grass Valley [Nevada]. The post office was established in
1850 and called Centerville. Soon afterward it was changed
to the present descriptive name, which was then as unique
in the United States as Centerville was common. The valley
itself had been named Grassy Valley by the immigrants
who found here plenty of forage for their half-starved
cattle.

Great Basin. The region of Nevada, western Utah, and southeastern California was so called by Frémont because its
streams lost themselves in the basin.

Great Western Divide. The ridge between the headwaters of
the Kern and Kaweah rivers was named by J. N. LeConte
in 1896.

Gridley [Butte]. The station was named by the Southern Pacific in 1870 for George W. Gridley, owner of the land on
which it was built.

Griffith Park [Los Angeles]. Named by the city council in
1896, for Griffith J. Griffith, donor of the park area.

Grizzly. Over one hundred places, almost all in the high
mountains, are named for the grizzly bear, now extinct
but once important in California lore.

Groveland [Tuolumne]. The popular American place name
was given to the community in the 1850's, replacing the
old name, First Garrote (first execution, i.e., hanging).

Guadelupe, gwah-da-loop'-ee, gwah-da-loop'. The name of
the patron saint of Catholic Mexico, the Virgin of Guadalupe, was extremely popular as a place name in Spanish
California. The river in Santa Clara County was named
by the Anza expedition in 1776; the names in Santa Barbara and San Mateo counties came from land grants.

Guajome, wah-hoh'-may [San Diego]. A Spanish rendering of
a Luiseño Indian place name, possibly meaning 'frog.' It

was the name of a grant conveyed to two Indians in 1845.

Gualala, wah-lah′-lah [Sonoma]. A Spanish phonetic rendering of Walhalla, in Teutonic mythology the abode of heroes fallen in battle. The form Walhalla (variously spelled) was applied by Ernest Rufus, grantee of Rancho German in 1846, either directly because of the romantic setting, or indirectly because the name of the Indian village there sounded like the German word to him.

Guatay, gwah′-tye [San Diego]. The name is derived from the Diegueño Indian word *kwatai* (large).

Guerneville [Sonoma]. The post office was named in the 1870′s for George Guerne, who had built a sawmill here in 1864.

Gustine [Merced]. Laid out in the 1890′s and named for Augustine, daughter of Henry Miller, of Miller & Lux, California cattle barons.

Hackamore [Modoc]. A Western term (from *jáquima*) for a halter used in breaking horses. The station was named Jaquima in 1910 and the spelling was changed in 1928.

Haiwee, hay′-way [Inyo]. An Indian name for dove, *haiwai*, was recorded as a place name in 1861.

Hamilton, Mount [Santa Clara]. Named for the Rev. Laurentine Hamilton, who with Brewer and Hoffmann, of the Whitney Survey, climbed to the top on August 26, 1861.

Hanaupah [Death Valley]. The name was perhaps derived from *honopi*, a Panamint Indian word for canyon.

Hanford [Kings]. The station was named in 1877, for James Hanford, treasurer of the Central Pacific R.R.

Hangtown Creek [El Dorado]. Preserves the nickname of Placerville, so called in the 1850′s because of the speedy dispatch of several robbers in 1849.

Harbin [Lake]. James M. Harbin, immigrant of 1846, settled at the springs about 1857.

Havasu Lake, hav′-a-soo [San Bernardino]. This artificial lake was given the Mojave Indian name for 'blue' in 1939.

Havilah [Kern]. Named in 1864 after the Biblical gold land, mentioned in Genesis 2:2.

Hawthorne [Los Angeles]. The community was named, about 1906, for the great American novelist.

Hayward [Alameda]. The town was laid out in 1854 and named for William Hayward, owner of the hotel.

Healdsburg [Sonoma]. The post office was named in 1857 for Harmon G. Heald, a pioneer of 1846.

Hecker Pass [Santa Clara]. Named in 1928 for Henry Hecker, who was instrumental in building the highway across it.

Hedionda Creek [Santa Clara]. The Spanish word for 'fetid' or 'stinking' was often applied to malodorous creeks.

Hemet [Riverside]. The name, applied before 1900, may be Indian or derived from Swedish *hemmet* (in the home).

Henness Pass [Nevada]. Known since 1850 by this name; Patrick Henness was a trail blazer of the route.

Hermosa Beach [Los Angeles]. The Spanish adjective for 'beautiful' was given to the subdivision in 1901.

Hetch Hetchy [Yosemite N. P.]. The valley has been known by this name since the early 1860's. The Indian words apparently mean either edible seeds or acorns.

Hetten or **Ketten** [Trinity]. The Wintun Indian word for 'camas,' or wild hyacinth.

Hilgard, Mount [Fresno]. Named in 1896 for Professor E. W. Hilgard, pioneer of scientific agriculture in California.

Hillsborough [San Mateo]. Incorporated in 1910 and named after Hillsboro, New Hampshire, the ancestral home of the owner of the property.

Hobart Mills [Nevada]. Named in 1897 for Walter Scott Hobart, pioneer lumberman.

Hoffmann, Mount [Yosemite N. P.]. Named by the Whitney Survey in 1863 for Charles Hoffmann, native of Germany and topographer of the survey throughout its existence. The mountain in Modoc County was named for his brother John; the one in Lassen National Park, for his son George.

Hollister [San Benito]. Named in 1868 for Colonel W. W. Hollister, owner of San Justo Rancho, on which the town was established. The name San Justo was first suggested but lost out when a citizen voiced a loud protest against adding to the long list of saints in the state.

Hollywood [Los Angeles]. Named in 1886, probably after one of the Hollywoods "back East," but possibly after the toyon, popularly known as California holly.

Homers Nose [Sequoia N. P.]. Jestingly named by surveyors in 1872 because the mountain looked like the nose of Joseph Homer, who was with the surveying party.

Honcut [Butte]. A Maidu Indian village name, applied to a grant in 1844 and to the post office in the 1880's.

Hondo, hon'-doh. The Spanish adjective for 'deep' has become a place name by itself; the masculine gender, *hondo,* was formerly used with the masculine words *arroyo* (creek) and *río* (river); the feminine *honda,* with *cañada* (valley or glen) and *laguna* (lagoon or lake).

Honey Lake [Lassen]. So named before 1850 because of the sweetish substance deposited on the plants by the honey-dew aphis and valued by the Indians as a food.

Hoopa [Humboldt]. The name for the natives on the lower course of Trinity River was recorded in 1852.

Hopland [Mendocino]. Called Sanel until 1880 when a successful experiment at growing hops gave the new name.

Hornitos [Mariposa]. The place was occupied by Mexican miners in 1852, and was probably named after Los Hornitos, Durango, Mexico. Hornitos is a diminutive of *horno,* 'bake oven,' but none of the different versions of its origin has been proved.

Horse. Some of the physical features so named go back to the 1840's and 1850's when large herds of wild horses (the ancestors of which had escaped from the missions) roamed through the country.

Horse Linto Creek, hoss-lin'-ten [Humboldt]. A popular version for the Hoopa Indian village recorded as *Has-lintah* in 1852.

Huasna, wahz'-na [San Luis Obispo]. The name of a Chumash Indian village was preserved in creek and river and in the title of a land grant in 1843.

Hueneme, wy-nee'-ma, wy-nee'-mee [Ventura]. The name is derived from the Chumash Indian village *Wene'-me;* the point was named by the Coast Survey in 1856.

Huerhuero, wehr-o-wehr'-o [San Luis Obispo]. This was the name of a land grant of 1842. The name may have an Indian root, or it may be from Mexican *huero,* 'putrid.'

Humboldt. The name of the German scientist and traveler, Alexander von Humboldt, was given to the bay by officers of the *Laura Virginia,* which entered the port in April, 1850. The county was named after the bay in 1853.

Humphreys, Mount [Fresno]. Named by the Whitney Survey for A. A. Humphreys, distinguished engineer and soldier.

Hungry Bill Ranch [Death Valley]. Hungry Bill, a Panamint Indian, received the ranch for services in the Modoc War.

Huntington. The places in Los Angeles, Orange, and Fresno counties commemorate the industrial leader, Henry E. Huntington, who will be best remembered as the donor of the Huntington Library and Art Gallery at San Marino.

Hurdygurdy [Del Norte]. The name goes back to the mining days when the Hurdygurdy water wheel and the Hurdygurdy girls were extremely popular. Many diggings and camps were so named.

Hynes [Los Angeles]. The post office was named in 1907 for C. B. Hynes of the Salt Lake Railroad.

Iaqua, eye'-a-kway [Humboldt]. The origin of the name may have been *aiekwi,* 'good day,' a native greeting still heard in the county. Camp Iaqua is recorded in 1864.

Ibex [Death Valley]. Named for the desert bighorn sheep, often called ibex.

Idria, id'-ree-a [San Benito]. Named after the New Idria quicksilver mine, which had been named in the 1850's after a famous quicksilver mine on the Adriatic Sea.

Ignacio [Marin]. In 1840 Ignacio Pacheco was grantee of the land on which the town is situated.

Igo [Shasta]. Probably an Indian name applied in the late 1870's. Popular legend connects the name with near-by Ono and derives the names from a conversation between a boy (or a Chinaman) and an adult: "I go, I go." "Oh, no! Oh, no!" Igo and Ono occur also in San Bernardino County within twenty miles of each other.

Illilouette, il-lil'-oo-et' [Yosemite N. P.]. Members of the Whitney Survey are responsible for the application of the queer name, apparently the result of a misunderstanding.

Imperial Valley. An imposing name applied to the southern part of Colorado Desert in 1906 when the California Development Company reclaimed the region for colonization.

Independence. A favorite American place name, found in the names of at least twelve California places and features. Independence [Inyo] was named in 1866 after a military camp, established on Independence Day, July 4, 1862. Independence Lake [Nevada] was named by the actress Lola Montez on a Fourth of July in the early 1850's.

Indio [Riverside]. The Spanish for 'Indian' was given to the Southern Pacific station in the late 1870's.

Inglewood [Los Angeles]. Founded in 1887 and named by a visitor from Inglewood, Canada.

Inverness [Marin]. Named in 1889 after Inverness, Scotland, the birthplace of one of the founders.

Inyo. The first party to attempt mining in the district in 1860 was told by the Indians that the mountain range was called Inyo, meaning 'dwelling place of a great spirit.' The county was named in 1866.

Ione [Amador]. The mining town is mentioned in 1853. It is not known whether it was named after Ione, Illinois, or for one of Bulwer-Lytton's heroines.

Irvine [Orange]. In 1870 James Irvine purchased Rancho San Joaquin and established his orchards. The University was established in 1965.

Irvington [Alameda]. The post office was named in 1884. As the place had formerly been Washington Corners, association with the name of Washington Irving is indicated.

Islais Creek [San Francisco]. *Islay* was the Salinan Indian name for the native hollyleaf cherry, mentioned since 1775 and found in place names where the shrub thrived.

Isleton [Sacramento]. The unique name, coined from "isle," was given to the town built on Andrus Island in 1874.

Ivanhoe [Tulare]. Named in 1924 after the school district, which had been named in 1885 for Walter Scott's novel.

Ivanpah [San Bernardino]. The name, meaning 'good water' in Southern Piute, was applied to the terminal of the Santa Fe branch from Goffs in 1902.

Jackson [Amador]. This name and Jacksonville [Tuolumne] honor "Colonel" Alden M. Jackson, a lawyer, generally liked by the miners for settling quarrels out of court.

Jacumba, hah-kum'-ba [San Diego]. A rancheria, *Jacom*, appears in 1795; *la sierra de Jacum* in 1841. The word may be Diegueño Indian, with the original stem *aha*, 'water.'

Jalama, ha-lam'-a [Santa Barbara]. Named after a Chumash Indian rancheria of La Purisima Mission in 1791.

Jamacha, ham'-a-shaw [San Diego]. A rancheria *Xamacha* was mentioned in 1775; a land grant *Jamacha* is recorded in 1831. The spelling of the Geographic Board is Jamacao. The name is probably derived from Diegueño Indian *hamacha,* a small wild squash.

Jamestown [Tuolumne]. The mining town was named for George F. James, of San Francisco, and appears on maps since 1852. The local nickname is "Jimtown."

Jamul, ha-mool' [San Diego]. A Diegueño Indian word meaning 'foam' or 'lather.' The place is mentioned as *Jamol* in 1776 and as *Jamul* in the 1820's.

Jayhawker Well [Death Valley]. Applied by the National Park Service in 1936; the Jayhawker party from Illinois, which crossed the desert in 1849, had camped there.

Jenny Lind [Calaveras]. The mining town was named for the "Swedish nightingale," whose tour of Eastern cities in 1850–1852 excited the country.

Jim Crow Canyon [Sierra]. A Kanaka, called Jim Crow as Kanakas frequently were, is said to have returned with supplies from Sacramento and found his employers gone. He worked the claim alone and struck it rich. .

Jobs Peak, Jobs Sister [Alpine]. Known as "Job's peaks" in the early 1850's when Moses Job had a store in Sheridan.

Johannesburg [Kern]. Named in 1897 after the famous mining center in South Africa. The town is popularly known as Joburg.

Jolon, ho-lohn′ [Monterey]. The place, probably a Salinan
Indian rancheria, was recorded in the early 1800's. The
name was applied to the post office about 1860.

Jordan, Mount [Tulare]. Named by the Sierra Club in 1925,
in honor of David Starr Jordan, president of Stanford
University, 1891 to 1916.

Joshua Tree National Monument. The desert tree (*Yucca
brevifolia*) was named by the Mormons, to whom it seemed
a symbol of Joshua leading them to a promised land.

Judah, Mount [Placer]. Named in 1941 by the Sierra Club;
it belatedly honors the construction engineer, Theodore D.
Judah, guiding spirit in the building of the Central Pacific
across the Sierra.

Junipero Serra Peak, huh-nip′-er-oh [Monterey]. Junípero
Serra founded nine missions in Alta California during his
presidency from 1769 to 1784. The name was applied to
the highest peak of the Santa Lucia Mountains in 1907.

Jurupa Mountains, huh-roop′-a [San Bernardino, Riverside].
An Indian word of unknown meaning. It was applied to
two land grants in 1838.

Kaiser [Fresno]. The name for peak, pass, ridge, and other
features goes back to Kaiser or Keyser Gulch of early mining days. Perhaps it was named originally for Richard
Keyes, a successful miner of 1853, and the present version
may have arisen through a misunderstanding. It is also
possible that this was the place where Elijah Keyser, of
Pennsylvania, struck it rich in the gold rush.

Kanaka, ka-nak′-a. A number of places bear this popular
name for Hawaiian Islanders, some of whom were in California long before the gold rush.

Kangaroo. The name was applied in several northern counties, probably because of the presence of kangaroo rats.

Kaweah, kah-wee′-ah [Tulare]. The river system was known
in 1851 as Four Creeks, the first of which, Cowier or Cah-
wia, was named for the Yokuts Indian tribe or village on
its bank. In 1853 the name, spelled Kaweeyah, was given
to all four branches.

Kearsarge [Fresno, Inyo]. In 1863 Southerners named the range north of Owens Lake in honor of the Confederate raider *Alabama.* When the vessel was sunk by the *Kearsarge* in 1864, Union men called their claims Kearsarge Mining District.

Keeler [Inyo]. Named in 1882 for J. M. Keeler, manager of a nearby marble quarry. He was a forty-niner.

Keene [Kern]. Named in 1879 for the Keene family.

Keith, Mount [Inyo]. Named in 1896 for William Keith, a native of Scotland and well-known painter.

Kekawaka [Trinity]. A local Indian word, possibly meaning 'frog creek.'

Kelseyville [Lake]. Named Kelsey Town in the 1860's in memory of Andrew Kelsey, killed by the Indians in 1849 in revenge for his mistreatment of them.

Kentfield [Marin]. Named in 1905 for Albert E. Kent, who had built his home here in 1872.

Kerckhoff Dome [Fresno]. Named for William G. Kerckhoff, of Los Angeles, a promoter and philanthropist.

Kern. The river was named by Frémont in 1845, for his topographer and artist, Edward M. Kern, of Philadelphia. The county was named in 1866.

Kettleman Hills [Kings]. Dave Kettleman was a 'forty-niner and a pioneer cattleman of the county.

Kiavah Mountain [Kern]. Named for a Piute chief.

Kibesillah [Mendocino]. Probably a Pomo Indian name meaning 'flat rock.'

Kimshew Creek [Butte]. Probably from Maidu Indian *ki-wim se'-u* (little water).

King City [Monterey]. The station was named by the Southern Pacific in 1886, for C. H. King, owner of Rancho San Lorenzo.

Kings River. The river was named *Rio de los Santos Reyes* in 1805 by Gabriel Moraga because it was discovered on Epiphany, the day of the three holy kings. The present name appeared on maps in 1850.

Kirker: Pass, Creek [Contra Costa]. Named for "Don Santiago" Kirker, Indian fighter, who died here in 1852.

Klamath River. The name of an Indian tribe and a river in the region was mentioned as *Clammitt* in 1826; Rogue River was called *Clamouth* in 1828. The name appeared in various spellings on maps and in records until the present version was established when the now defunct Klamath County was created in 1851.

Knights Landing [Yolo], **Knights Ferry** [Stanislaus]. Both places commemorate William Knight, of Indiana, who settled on the Sacramento in 1843, and after the discovery of gold operated a ferry on the Stanislaus.

Koip Peak [Mono]. Named by the Geological Survey in 1883. *Koipa* means 'mountain sheep' in Northern Piute Indian dialect.

Konocti, kon-ok′-tye, **Mount** [Lake]. The name is derived from Southeastern Pomo Indian *kno* (mountain) and *hatai* (woman). Also known as Uncle Sam Mountain.

Kuna Peak [Mono]. Applied by the Geological Survey in 1883. *Kuna* means 'firewood' in the Mono Indian dialect.

Kyburz [El Dorado]. Named for Albert Kyburz, son of Samuel Kyburz, a native of Switzerland, who was an important figure at Sutter's Fort before and during the gold rush.

La Canada, kan yad′ ah [Los Angeles]. The name, meaning 'valley' or 'glen,' is derived from a land grant of 1843 called *La Cañada*. *See* **Cañada.**

La Crescenta [Los Angeles]. An artificial name with a Romanic touch, applied to the post office in 1888.

Lafayette [Contra Costa]. The settlement was named in 1853; like the many other Lafayettes in the United States, it honors the French general who fought in the American War for Independence.

La Grange [Stanislaus]. The name of Lafayette's country seat, a favorite place name in America, was applied to the place when it was made county seat in 1856.

Laguna, Lagunita. The Spanish words for 'lake' (or 'lagoon') and 'little lake' have survived in many place names. In American times they were often applied without regard to meaning: Lake Laguna means 'lake lake.'

La Habra, hah'-bra [Orange]. The place name was preserved through a land grant dated October 22, 1839, which in turn probably derived its name from *abra*, 'canyon,' 'gorge.'

La Jolla, hoy'-a [San Diego]. The word, also spelled *Joya* or *Hoya* (hollow, cavity, pit, or river bed), is a Mexican geographical term, repeatedly found in Spanish California documents and maps. The name in San Diego County was probably first applied to a hollow, or to a rancheria "in the hollow"; it appears in mission and land-grant records since 1828, and was applied to the town in 1869.

Lake County. Created in 1861 and so named because Clear Lake is the principal physical feature within the county.

Lamanda Park [Los Angeles]. The name was coined in 1886 by Leonard J. Rose by prefixing the initial letter of his given name to his wife's name, Amanda.

La Mesa [San Diego]. The name was first used in 1886 as La Mesa Heights. *See* Mesa.

La Mirada [Los Angeles]. Given to the Santa Fe station in 1888. A Spanish noun, *mirada,* means 'glance,' 'gaze.'

Lancha Plana [Amador]. The historic landmark recalls the mining town of the 1850's, so named because a flatboat (*lancha plana*) was used here as a ferry.

Langley, Mount [Inyo]. Named in 1905 in honor of Samuel P. Langley, astronomer and physicist. It has also been shown on maps as Mount Corcoran.

La Panza [San Luis Obispo]. So named because bear hunters used the belly (*panza*) of cattle as a bait.

Las Cruces [Santa Barbara]. The name, meaning 'the crosses,' goes back to a *Rancho de las Cruces* mentioned in 1822.

Las Flores. The Spanish name, 'the flowers,' was repeatedly used in Spanish times and is preserved in Tehama, San Diego, and Los Angeles counties.

Lassen. Peter Lassen, native of Denmark, came to California in 1840 and became the foremost pioneer of its northeastern section. The peak was known by his name before 1850; the county was named in 1864; the national forest in 1908; and Lassen Volcanic National Park in 1916, two years after the last eruption of the volcano.

Lassic, Mount [Trinity]. The name of an Indian tribe, whose chief was called Lassik.

Lava Beds National Monument [Modoc, Siskiyou]. Created and named in 1925. The name became well known after the Indians had used the lava beds as a stronghold in the Modoc War of 1872–1873.

La Verne [Los Angeles]. Named in 1916 after La Verne Heights, which had been named for the promoter.

Lavigia Hill [Santa Barbara]. The Spanish name for 'lookout' was applied by the Coast Survey in the 1850's.

Lebec [Kern]. Peter Lebeck was killed here by a grizzly in 1837. His name was preserved through an inscription on an oak, first mentioned in 1847.

LeConte. The falls in Tuolumne, the peak in Inyo, and the divide in Fresno County were named for Joseph LeConte, geologist and mountaineer; the canyon in Fresno and the point in Tuolumne County were named for his son, Joseph Nisbet LeConte, also a well-known mountaineer.

Leevining, lee-vy′-ning [Mono]. Named for Leroy Vining, of Indiana, who came to California in 1852 and later operated a sawmill at the creek.

Lembert Dome [Yosemite N. P.]. In 1885 John B. Lembert took up a homestead near the glaciated dome.

Lemoore [Kings]. The place was known as Lee Moore's, for Dr. L. Lee Moore, until the Southern Pacific used the present form for its station in the 1880's.

Lennox [Los Angeles]. Named before 1921 after Lenox, Massachusetts, former home of an early resident.

Leucadia [San Diego]. The name of one of the Ionian Islands was given to the town by English settlers in 1885.

Lick Observatory [Santa Clara]. James Lick, a Pennsylvania German, real-estate speculator, and public benefactor, gave the observatory to the University of California.

Likely [Modoc]. The story is told that when the settlers tried to find a name for the post office in 1878, one of them remarked, "Wa'al, we're likely to find a name and we're likely not to." The emphasis on the adverb captured the group's fancy and they selected it as the name.

Lindo, Linda. The Spanish adjective for 'pretty' is repeatedly found in place names. Linda [Yuba], however, was named in 1850 after the first steamer launched on Sacramento River.

Lindsay [Tulare]. Applied to the Southern Pacific station in 1888 for Mrs. A. J. Hutchinson, née Lindsay.

Livermore [Alameda]. Robert Livermore, an English sailor, came to California in the 1820's and settled in the valley which now bears his name. Post office and railroad station were named in his memory in 1869.

Llagas Creek, yah'-gas [Santa Clara]. Named *Las Llagas de Nuestro Padre San Francisco* (the wounds of our father Saint Francis) by Palou in 1774.

Llanada, la-nad'-ah [San Benito]. The Spanish word for 'plain' or 'level ground.'

Llano, ya'-noh [Los Angeles]. Named after the socialistic colony, Llano del Rio (plain of the river), 1914 to 1917.

Lobos, Lobitos. The Spanish words for 'wolves' and 'little wolves' are preserved in various places. The points on the coast, Point Lobos [San Francisco], Point Lobos State Park [Monterey], Lobitos Creek [San Mateo], really refer to the *lobo marino* (sea wolf, seal).

Loco [Inyo]. The station was named in 1910 for a division of Mono Indians, called Loko.

Lodi, loh'-dye [San Joaquin]. Named in 1874, probably for one of the twenty other Lodis then existing in the United States. A famous race horse of the 1870's was called "Lodi"; this may have influenced the naming.

Lola, Mount [Nevada]. Named for the actress and dancer, Lola Montez, a colorful figure in the early 1850's.

Loma, Lomita. The Spanish word for 'low hill' and its diminutive form are still actively used, often without regard to meaning, for mountains as well as subdivisions.

Lompoc, lom'-pohk [Santa Barbara]. The name of a Chumash Indian rancheria, probably for 'shell mound,' mentioned as early as 1791, was applied to the town in 1874.

Long Beach [Los Angeles]. This descriptive name was applied to the development in the boom year, 1887.

Los Altos [Santa Clara]. The Spanish term, 'the heights,' was given to the post office in 1908, after the subdivision so named in 1907.

Los Angeles, an'-je-les, ang'-gless. The river was named *Rio de Porciuncula* by the Portolá expedition, August 2, 1769, for it was the day of *Nuestra Señora de los Angeles de Porciúncula* (Our Lady of the Angels of Portiuncula). Portiuncula was the chapel in Assisi, Italy, cradle of the Franciscan Order. The full name of the river was recorded by Palou, December 10, 1773. The *pueblo* was founded in 1781 with the name *Reina de los Angeles,* but almost invariably appeared on maps and often in documents as Pueblo de Los Angeles. Various forms of the name were used ("City of the Angels" in 1847!) until the county and city became officially Los Angeles in 1850.

Los Banos [Merced]. The original settlement was established by Gustav Kreyenhagen some time after 1868, and named after Los Banos Creek. The latter had apparently been named in Spanish times *Arroyo de los Baños* (creek of the baths) because the pools at the head of the creek had been used for bathing.

Los Coches, koh'-ches [Santa Barbara]. Named in Mexican times for herds of wild hogs that had escaped from the mission.

Los Gatos, los gat'-os [Santa Clara]. The creek and the ridge were named *de los Gatos* (of the [wild] cats) in Spanish times, and in 1840 the name was given to a land grant. The post office was named Los Gatos in 1864.

Los Nietos, nee-eh'-tos [Los Angeles]. Valley and town doubtless commemorate the name of Manuel Nieto, in 1784 grantee of the large Nieto grant, regranted to his five heirs (*los Nietos*) in 1834.

Los Padres National Forest. Named in 1936 to commemorate the Franciscan padres, eight of whose missions are in or near the forest reserve.

Los Penasquitos Canyon, pen-as-kee'-tos [San Diego]. The name, meaning 'small rocks,' appears in the land grant, *Santa Maria de los Peñasquitos,* June 15, 1823.

Lost Hills [Kern]. In 1910 the town was named after the Lost Hills, slight elevations which seem to belong to the Kettleman Hills but look as if they were "lost."

Lost Wagons [Death Valley]. Some wagons of a borax company were abandoned here in 1889.

Lowe, Mount [Los Angeles]. Named for Thaddeus S. C. Lowe by his companions on the first horseback ascent, September 24, 1892. Lowe was a well-known engineer and inventor.

Lucerne. The name of the medieval town and beautiful lake in Switzerland, the site of Wilhelm Tell's exploits, is repeatedly used as a place name in California. Some names, like Lucerne Valley [San Bernardino], were, however, derived from the European word for alfalfa.

Ludlow [San Bernardino]. Named in the 1870's by the railroad for William B. Ludlow, master car repairer.

Lukens Lake [Yosemite N. P.]. Named in 1894 for Theodore P. Lukens, mayor of Pasadena at that time.

Luther Pass [El Dorado, Alpine]. Named for Ira M. Luther, who crossed the pass in a wagon in 1854 and later advocated routing the Central Pacific across the pass.

Lyell, Mount [Yosemite N. P.]. Named by the Whitney Survey in 1863 for Charles Lyell, noted English geologist.

Lynwood [Los Angeles]. Named for Lynn Wood Sessions, wife of the owner of a local dairy.

McCloud River [Siskiyou, Shasta]. The name honored Alexander McLeod of the Hudson's Bay Company. In the 1850's it was associated with a pioneer settler, Ross McCloud.

McClure, Lake [Mariposa]. Named in 1927 in memory of Wilbur F. McClure, State Engineer, 1912–1926.

McDuffie, Mount [Kings Canyon N. P.]. Named in 1951 for Duncan McDuffie, mountaineer and conservationist.

McGee. The McGee creeks and other features in Mono and Inyo counties were named for the four McGee brothers, pioneer cattlemen of the district.

McLaren. The park in San Francisco and the meadows in Contra Costa County are named in honor of John McLaren, who was superintendent of San Francisco parks, 1890–1943.

Maclure, Mount [Madera]. Named in 1868 after William Maclure, native of Scotland, pioneer of American geology.

Madera, ma-dehr'-a [Madera]. The Spanish name for wood, timber, and lumber was applied to the lumber town at the terminus of a water flume in 1876. The county was created in 1893 and named after the town.

Mad River [Humboldt, Trinity]. Named in December, 1849, by members of the Gregg party; their leader, Dr. Josiah Gregg, became terribly "mad" when they refused to wait for him to take the latitude of the river's mouth.

Madrone. The common name for one of California's most beautiful native trees is derived from the Spanish *madroño* (strawberry tree) and is found in many place names.

Malibu [Los Angeles]. The origin of the name is probably the Chumash Indian rancheria *Umalibo* in the jurisdiction of Mission San Buenaventura. The present spelling is found as early as 1805 in the Topanga Malibu land grant.

Mallory, Mount [Inyo, Tulare]. Named in 1925, in memory of George Mallory, a member of the British Mount Everest expedition, who lost his life in June, 1924, after reaching a height of 28,000 feet.

Malpaso Canyon [Monterey]. *Arroyo de mal paso* (creek of tough going) was recorded in 1835. The name is also found in Mendocino and Humboldt counties.

Manhattan Beach [Los Angeles]. Named in 1902 after Manhattan Island, New York.

Manly Peak [Death Valley]. William Lewis Manly played a heroic role in a crossing of Death Valley in 1849.

Manteca, man-tee'-ka [San Joaquin]. The Southern Pacific named the station in 1870, after a local creamery which was appropriately named *Manteca* (butter).

Manzanita, man-za-nee'-ta. The name of the beautiful native shrub, meaning literally 'little apple' in Spanish, is found in some fifty place names.

Mare Island [Solano]. The island, now part of a peninsula, became known about 1840 as *Isla de la Yegua* (Mare Island), apparently because one of Vallejo's mares had found her way there and joined a herd of elk.

Maricopa [Kern]. When the Southern Pacific built the extension from Sunset (Monarch) in 1904, the terminus was called Maricopa, apparently for the Indian tribe on the Gila River in Arizona.

Marin, ma-rin'. According to tradition, the name was first applied to the larger Marin Island in Mexican times for an Indian of Mission San Rafael who lived on it. Since the bay in which the islands lie was called *Bahia de . . . la Marinera* in 1775, the name may actually have been derived from this early name. It was applied to the county in 1850.

Mariposa. A place in this general region was called *Mariposas* (butterflies) by a Spanish expedition in 1806, because the soldiers encountered multitudes of them. The county was created and named on February 18, 1850; it first included all territory between Tuolumne and Los Angeles counties and between the Coast Ranges and Nevada.

Markleeville [Alpine]. The post office was named in 1864 for Jacob J. Marklee, settler of 1861.

Marshall Monument [El Dorado]. The monument was erected by the state in 1890, in honor of James W. Marshall, the discoverer of gold at Sutter's mill in January, 1848.

Marsh Creek [Contra Costa]. The only feature which preserves the name of John Marsh, of Massachusetts, one of the foremost pioneers of central California, who settled at the foot of Mount Diablo in 1838.

Martinez, mar-tee'-nes [Contra Costa]. Named in 1849, for Ignacio Martínez, *comandante* at the presidio of San Francisco, 1822–1827; grantee in 1829 of Rancho El Pinole, on which the town was built.

Marysville [Yuba]. The town was laid out in 1849–1850 by Charles Covillaud and associates, and named for Mary Murphy Covillaud, a survivor of the Donner Party and wife of the principal owner.

Massacre Canyon [Riverside]. So named because the Temecula Indians here massacred a band of Ivahs for the possession of a supply of wild grain.

Mather, math'-er. The pass in Fresno, the station in Tuolumne, and the grove in Humboldt counties were named for

Stephen T. Mather, native of San Francisco and first Director of the National Park Service (1917–1929).

Matilija, ma-til'-i-hah [Ventura]. Named after a Chumash Indian rancheria, *Matilja,* mentioned in early records of Mission San Buenaventura. The matilija poppy was so named because it grew profusely in the canyon.

Matterhorn Peak [Yosemite N. P.]. The name was applied in 1878, apparently with too much imagination, for it bears little resemblance to the peak in Switzerland.

Mattole River, mat-tohl' [Humboldt]. After the name of an Athapascan tribe who resisted the white man most vigorously and were practically exterminated. Local tradition interprets the name to mean originally 'clear water.'

Maturango Peak [Inyo]. The name is recorded in the early 1870's by the Wheeler Survey, but its meaning is unknown.

Mayacmas Mountains, may-yack'-mas. The range west of Clear Lake bears the name of a former Indian village near Calistoga, *Miyakmah,* a name which was preserved through the land grant Mallacomes of 1841.

Mecca [Riverside]. The only one of several Meccas in the United States which resembles the Arabian city in climate and surroundings. Named in 1905.

Melones [Calaveras]. The post office was not established until 1902, but the name goes back to early mining days.

Mendocino, men-doh-see'-noh. The origin of the name and its application to the cape in latitude 40°26' is shrouded in obscurity. It has appeared on maps since 1587. It is quite generally assumed to have been named in honor of Lorenzo Suárez de Mendoza, viceroy of New Spain, 1580–1583, although it might have been named earlier and in honor of Antonio de Mendoza, a former viceroy of New Spain. The county, one of the original twenty-seven, was created and named in 1850.

Mendota [Fresno]. The station was named in 1895, and, like many other railroad stations, was probably named after one of the Mendotas "back East."

Menlo Park [San Mateo]. Named in 1854 by settlers from Ireland, after Menlough, county Galway, Ireland.

Merced, mer-sed'. The names in Merced and Mariposa counties go back to the *Rio de Nuestra Señora de la Merced* (river of our lady of mercy) applied by Gabriel Moraga on September 29, 1806.

Merced, Lake [San Francisco]. The lake was named *Laguna de Nuestra Señora de la Merced* on September 24, 1775, the feast day of Our Lady of Mercy.

Meridian [Sutter]. The name was given to the post office in 1860 because of its proximity to the Mount Diablo meridian.

Merritt, Lake [Alameda]. Through the efforts of Mayor Samuel B. Merritt the slough was made a lake in 1869. It received its name in 1891.

Mesa, may'-sa. The Spanish word for a flat-topped hill is generally used in the American southwest but it has not replaced the corresponding English 'table hill.' There are more than twenty mesas in the state, together with a number of towns so named: La Mesa, Mesa Grande, Mesaville.

Mesquite, mes-keet'. The mesquite tree, from the Aztec word *mizquitl,* is found in arid regions of Mexico and is valued for its nutritious beans. In California, where it occurs in Death Valley and south of it, it has given its name to a number of places.

Middletown [Lake]. Named in the 1860's when it was a stage stop halfway between Lower Lake and Calistoga.

Millbrae [San Mateo]. Applied to the railroad station in the 1860's after the country place of Darius O. Mills, a leading banker and promoter of San Francisco and New York.

Millerton Lake [Fresno, Madera]. The reservoir covers the site of Millerton, named in 1854 after the near-by military post, Fort Miller.

Mill Valley [Marin]. The town of Mill Valley was not laid out until 1889, but the valley was long so known because of the sawmill built there in 1834 by John Reed.

Milpitas, mil-pee'-tas [Santa Clara]. Named after the Milpitas (Mexican, 'vegetable gardens') land grant of 1835. The name was first applied to the creek because one Martínez and some Indians had a truck garden there.

Miracle Hot Springs [Kern]. In 1947 this name was applied to Hobo Hot Springs.

Miramontes Point [San Mateo]. The Miramontes family, of San Francisco, settled in the vicinity in 1840.

Mission San Jose, san-o-zay′ [Alameda]. The post office was named in the 1860's after the mission which had been established in 1795 and dedicated to Saint Joseph.

Mi-Wuk Village [Tuolumne]. Named in 1955 after the nearby Miwok Indian village.

Moccasin [Tuolumne]. The name is shown for the creek on a map of 1852; it was probably applied because the miners mistook the water snakes for moccasin snakes.

Modesto [Stanislaus]. When in 1870 William C. Ralston, one of the directors of the Central Pacific, modestly declined to have his name used for the station, the Spanish adjective, meaning 'modest,' was chosen instead.

Modjeska [Orange]. Named for the Polish actress, Helena Modjeska, who lived in Orange County in the 1870's.

Modoc County, moh′-doc. The county was created in 1874, and named for the Indian tribe which had been subdued after severe fighting in the Modoc War of the preceding year. The word is derived from the Klamath Indian name *Moatokni,* 'people living south.'

Mohave, mo-hah′-ve [San Bernardino]. The place name, recorded with various spellings since the 17th century, was derived from that of an Indian tribe in the region where California, Arizona, and Nevada meet.

Mojave [Kern, Los Angeles, San Bernardino]. The names in the Great Basin arose because Frémont, in 1844, named the river for a group of roving Mohave Indians whom he met on April 23.

Mokelumne River, mo-kel′-um-ee. The name of the *Muguelemnes* [Indians] was mentioned in 1817; a *Rio Mokellemos* and Mogneles River were recorded in 1841 by the Wilkes party. The ending *-umni* means 'people,' hence 'people of Mokel,' a Miwok village near Lockeford.

Molino, mo-lee′-noh. The Spanish word for 'mill' survives in many place names. The corresponding term for the popular American millstream, or for mill creek, was *Arroyo de los Molinos;* hence several Molino Creeks.

Mono, Monache. The division of the Shoshonean Indians living on the eastern slope of the Sierra north of Owens Lake were called by their western neighbors *Monachi* (fly people) because their wealth consisted of the pupae of a fly found in great quantities at Mono and Owens lakes. The shorter form, Mono, was applied to the lake and to the northern Mono Pass in 1852 and to the county in 1861. The name Monache in Inyo County is recorded in 1864.

Monrovia [Los Angeles]. William N. Monroe, a railroad construction engineer, laid out the town in 1886.

Montalvo, mon-tal'-voh [Ventura]. The name of the Spanish author, in whose romance *Las Sergas de Esplandián* (about 1510) the name California was first used, was given to the station by the Southern Pacific in 1887.

Montara [San Mateo]. The name, spelled Montoro, was used for the mountain and the point by the Whitney Survey in 1867, and in 1869 the present form was used by the Coast Survey. Both are probably misspellings of one of several similar Spanish words referring to forest and mountain. A *Cañada Montosa* (valley full of woods and thickets) was shown, about 1838, on the map of San Pedro Rancho, on which peak, point, and town are situated.

Monte. The word means 'grove,' 'thicket,' or 'woods' in Spanish and is sometimes used to form pleasant-sounding but ungrammatical combinations for place names, like Monte Rio, Monte Vista, Miramonte. Although Spanish dictionaries list *monte* also with the meaning 'mountain,' it has rarely if ever been used as a geographical term with that meaning in Spanish-speaking countries.

Montebello [Los Angeles]. The name means 'beautiful mountain' in Italian and is of international currency. Until 1920 the town was known as Newmark for the Los Angeles pioneer, Harris Newmark.

Montecito [Santa Barbara]. The name means 'little grove' or 'woods.' It was mentioned as early as 1783, and was applied to a land grant in 1834.

Monterey. The bay was named in 1602 by Vizcaíno, in honor of the Count of Monterey, then viceroy of New Spain. The town developed around the presidio established by Portolá in 1770, the first Spanish military establishment in California. The county was created and named in 1850.

Montezuma. The name of the Aztec chief at the time of Cortez' invasion of Mexico was once a favorite place name. An attempt was made in 1827 to give this name to the province of Alta California.

Moraga Valley [Contra Costa]. Preserves the name of Joaquin Moraga, in 1835 co-grantee of the rancho on which station and valley are situated. He was probably the son of the explorer and soldier, Gabriel Moraga.

Moreno, mo-ree′-noh [Riverside]. Named in 1882 for one of the developers, F. E. Brown, whose name was translated into Spanish after he refused to permit the use of his name.

Morgan Hill [Santa Clara]. Named in 1892 for Morgan Hill, on whose ranch the settlement developed.

Mormon. The many place names go back to early days when members of the Mormon church played an important role in the Mexican War, the gold rush, and the early settlement of the state.

Moro Rock [Sequoia N. P.]. *Moro* is a word used by Mexican Californians for 'blue roan.' The rock is named for a mustang that often ranged up under the rock.

Morongo [Riverside]. The names for pass and valley, recorded since the 1850's, are derived from a Shoshonean village.

Morrison, Mount [Mono]. Named for Robert Morrison, of Benton, who was killed at Convict Lake, beneath the mountain, by escaped convicts on September 24, 1871.

Morro [San Luis Obispo]. The names of the region are derived from Morro Rock at the entrance of the bay, first mentioned by Crespi, September 8, 1769. The name *Morro,* a common Spanish term for a round rock or round-topped hill, is also found in Ventura and San Diego counties.

Mother Lode. In early mining days it was falsely assumed that a huge vein of gold-bearing quartz extended from the

American River to a point near Mariposa, and that the known veins were offsprings of this 'mother lode.'

Mount Bullion [Mariposa]. Named in 1850 after the eminence on Frémont's ranch to which Frémont had given this name. "Old Bullion" was the nickname of his father-in-law, Thomas Hart Benton, advocate of "hard money."

Mugu [Ventura]. Possibly the oldest recorded native name in the state, mentioned as an Indian village by Cabrillo in 1542. It probably means 'beach' in the Chumash dialect.

Muir. The great naturalist and mountaineer, John Muir (1838–1914), a native of Scotland, has been honored in more geographical names in California than any other individual. The best-known are: Muir Woods National Monument [Marin]; Muir Gorge [Yosemite N. P.]; John Muir Trail in the Sierra Nevada; Mount Muir [Sequoia N. P.].

Murieta. Joaquin Murieta was the John Doe for several Mexican bandits in the 1850's. The cave in Alameda County and the rocks in Fresno County were supposedly used by him for hideouts.

Muroc [Kern]. The Santa Fe named the station in 1910 by spelling backwards the family name of Clifford and Ralph Corum, homesteaders.

Murphys [Calaveras]. For John Murphy, immigrant of 1844, member of Charles Weber's mining company in 1848.

Murrieta [Riverside]. The post office was named in the 1880's for John Murrieta, ranch owner.

Nacimiento River, na-sim-ee-en'-toh [Monterey, San Luis Obispo]. *Nacimiento* means in Spanish 'source of a river' and Crespi of the Portolá expedition used it in this sense on September 21, 1769. Anza camped by the stream on April 16, 1774, and called it Nacimiento, assuming that it had been named for the Nativity (another meaning of the word). This name is found in records of 1795 and later years. The station was named after the river in 1905.

Napa, nap'-a. The name was recorded as *Napa* in 1823, for the plain so named by Indians who formerly lived there. The name was given to Salvador Vallejo's vast land grant in 1838, and to the county in 1850. It may be from the Indian word *napo* (house), recorded in 1851 in the Clear Lake region, or it may be from the Patwin Indian *napa* (grizzly bear).

Naranjo, na-ran'-hoh [Tulare]. The Spanish word for 'orange tree' was applied when the commercial growing of citrus fruits was begun in this region.

National City [San Diego]. Named in 1868 after the Rancho de la Nacion, on which the town was laid out. Until Mexican independence (1822) it had been called Rancho del Rey (the king's ranch).

Natoma, na-toh'-ma [Sacramento]. The post office was named about 1890. The name was used elsewhere as early as 1847. It probably contains either the Maidu Indian word *nato* (easterner) or *noto* (upstream).

Navalencia [Fresno]. The name, coined from the two leading orange varieties of the state, was applied to the Santa Fe station in 1913.

Navarro River [Mendocino]. Recorded in 1844 as Novarra or Novarro; probably a Spanish rendering of an Indian name.

Needham Mountain [Tulare]. Named for James C. Needham of Modesto, congressman from 1899 to 1913.

Needles [San Bernardino]. The railroad station, established in February, 1883, on the Arizona side of the Colorado River and named after the near-by pinnacles. The name was transferred to the California side in October.

Neenach [Los Angeles]. Apparently a Shoshonean Indian word, of unknown meaning and origin.

Negit Island [Mono Lake]. The Mono Indian word for 'blue-winged goose' was applied in 1882.

Nevada. This Spanish word meaning 'snow-covered,' or 'white as snow,' was applied to the town in 1850, and to the county and the waterfall in Yosemite in 1851. *See* Sierra Nevada.

Newark [Alameda]. Named in 1876 after Newark, New Jersey.

Newhall [Los Angeles]. The Southern Pacific station at the present site of Saugus was named in 1876 for Henry M. Newhall, the owner of the land. The name was moved to the present site in 1878.

Newman [Stanislaus]. Applied to the Southern Pacific station in 1887, for Simon Newman, local merchant.

Newport [Orange]. The McFadden brothers, who had come from Delaware, started a lumber business here in 1873, named their steamer *Newport* in 1876, and had the town-site of Newport platted in 1892.

New River [Imperial]. The name was applied by immigrants in 1849 when they came unexpectedly upon a stream which the expeditions of the preceding years had reported as a dry river bed and which was now filled by the overflow from the Colorado.

Nicasio, ni-kash'-oh [Marin]. The name was applied to a land grant in 1835 and again in 1844. It was derived from the name of a Christian Indian who had been baptized with the Spanish name of a saint.

Nicolaus, nick'-o-las [Sutter]. Named for Nicholaus Allgeier, a native of Germany, who operated a ferry on the Feather River at the time of the gold rush.

Nido, nee'-doh. The Spanish word for 'nest' is found in California place names in the sense of 'abode' or 'home.'

Niles [Alameda]. The station of the Central Pacific was named in 1869 for Judge Addison C. Niles, later of the California Supreme Court.

Nimshew [Butte]. A division of the Maidu Indians, Nemshaw, was recorded in 1841. The original meaning was probably 'big water.'

Nipomo, ni-poh'-moh [San Luis Obispo]. A Chumash Indian rancheria, *Nipoma,* was recorded in 1799. The present spelling was used in the name of a land grant in 1837.

Nojogui, nah'-hoh-wee [Santa Barbara]. The name may go back to a Chumash Indian name. It was mentioned as a rancheria in mission records.

Nomi-Lackee [Tehama]. A branch of Wintun Indians, forced to move west long before the coming of the white man and hence called *noam* (west) *lakki* (tongue or branch).

Nopah Range [Inyo]. Applied by the Geological Survey about 1910. *Pah* means 'water' in the Piute language, and the literal meaning may be 'no water range.'

Norco [Riverside]. Coined from *North Corona* Land Company in 1922. Lake Norconian is derived from Norco.

Norden [Nevada]. The post office was named after the lake, which had been named for Dr. Charles van Norden, of the South Yuba Water Company.

Nordhoff Peak [Ventura]. Applied by the Geological Survey in 1903 after the town of Nordhoff (now Ojai). Charles Nordhoff, the elder, was a writer who made the beauties of this California region known to the world.

Norwalk [Los Angeles]. The station was named in 1879. after the home town of settlers from Connecticut.

Novato, no-vah'-toh [Marin]. The name is found in *Cañada de Novato* mentioned in 1828, and in land grants of 1836 and 1839. It was probably the Spanish name of one of the Indian converts of Mission San Rafael.

Noyo River [Mendocino]. The name was transferred in the 1850's from the present Pudding Creek, which at that time bore the name of the Northern Pomo village *Noyo,* once. situated at its mouth.

Nubieber [Lassen]. When the extensions of the Great Northern and Western Pacific met in 1931 southwest of Bieber, the "new" station was named after the pioneer town.

Oakland [Alameda]. Because of the luxuriant growth of live oaks the site was called *Encinal* (oak grove) in Spanish times. The present name was spontaneously chosen when the city was laid out in 1850. Oakdale [Stanislaus], Oakville [Napa], Oakley [Contra Costa], Oak View Gardens [Ventura] and many other places were named after one of the fourteen varieties of oaks native to California.

Ocotillo [San Diego]. Named for the cactus-like plant. The name is derived from the Aztec root meaning 'prickly.'

Ojai, oh'-high [Ventura]. A rancheria Aujai is mentioned in mission records and with the spelling Ojai in land grant papers. A'hwai is Chumash for 'moon.'

Olancha [Inyo]. The Olanchas, a Shoshonean group south of Owens Lake, were mentioned in 1860. The peak was named by the Wheeler Survey in the 1870's.

Olema, oh-lee′-ma [Marin]. The name, applied to the post office in 1859, probably comes from a Hookooeko Indian word for the place. *Ole* is 'coyote' in Coast Miwok dialect. A rancheria *Olemos* is found in mission records after 1802.

Oleum [Contra Costa]. The name was coined in 1912 by lopping off the first four letters of petr*oleum*.

Olompali [Marin]. Olompali Indians were mentioned after 1816, and the name was used for a land grant in 1843.

Ono [Shasta]. The name of the Biblical town was chosen for the post office by the settlers in 1883. There is another Ono in San Bernardino County. *See* Igo.

Ontario [San Bernardino]. The town was laid out in 1882 by George B. Chaffey, who came from Ontario, Canada.

Ophir [Placer]. The only survivor of five mining towns named after Ophir, the gold land in the Bible.

Orange. The city was founded in 1873, and the county was created in 1889. The city was probably named to advertise one of the principal products of the district, although it may also have been named after one of the fifty-odd other Oranges in the United States.

Ord, Fort [Monterey]. Named by the War Department in 1933 for General Edward O. C. Ord, veteran of the Civil War, later commander of the Department of the Pacific.

Orestimba [Stanislaus]. *Arroyo de Orestimac* is mentioned in Spanish records in 1810. The present spelling was used for the name of a land grant in 1844. The name contains the Costanoan Indian name *ores* (bear).

Orick [Humboldt]. Recorded in 1852 as Oruk, the name given to the Redwood Creek Indians by the Indians living near the coast.

Orinda [Contra Costa]. Theodore Wagner, U. S. Surveyor General for California, applied the name Orinda Park in 1880 to his estate between Bear and Lauterwasser creeks; in 1895 the name was transferred to the village and in 1945 to the crossroads. The name may have been suggested by the pen name of the poet Katherine Phillips.

Orosi, oh-roh′-sye [Tulare]. The name, coined from the Spanish *oro* (gold), was given to the town in 1888.

Oroville [Butte]. The Post Office Department requested the renaming of Ophir City in 1855; the golden glimmer was preserved in a name coined from the Spanish word for gold.

Oso, oh'-soh. The Spanish name for 'bear' has survived as a place name in Stanislaus, Sutter, and San Luis Obispo counties. Oso Flaco (lean bear) Lake, in the latter county, was named *Laguna del Oso Flaco* by Portolá's soldiers.

Otay, oh'-tye [San Diego]. The name of a rancheria with the present spelling is mentioned as early as 1776. In 1829 and 1846 it was applied to a land grant and in 1849 to the river. It is a Diegueño Indian word meaning 'brushy.'

Owens Lake [Inyo]. Named by Frémont in 1845, for Richard Owens, of Ohio, a member of his third expedition.

Owenyo [Inyo]. Coined from Owens and Inyo in 1905 and applied to the new station in 1910.

Oxnard [Ventura]. Named for Henry T. Oxnard when he established a sugar refinery here in 1897.

Pacheco [Contra Costa]. Founded about 1858. Salvio Pacheco settled here on his Monte del Diablo Rancho in 1844.

Pacheco Pass [Santa Clara]. The pass, shown on the Frémont-Preuss map of 1848, was named for Francisco and Juan Pacheco, owners of ranchos.

Pacifica [San Mateo]. In 1957, nine communities incorporated as a city and chose the name in allusion to their situation along the ocean shore.

Paicines, py-see'-nes [San Benito]. The post office was named after the Indian village *Paisi-n* in 1874.

Pajaro River, pah'-ha-roh [Santa Cruz, Monterey]. The name (bird river) was applied to the stream by Portolá's soldiers in October, 1769. They found there an enormous bird which Indians had stuffed with straw.

Pala, pah'-lah [San Diego]. The place, probably a rancheria, is mentioned in 1781. The name may mean 'water' in Luiseño Shoshonean Indian.

Palm. The many place names containing the word were applied because of the occurrence of the native Washington palm or the Joshua palm.

Palo Alto, pal'-oh al'-toh [Santa Clara]. The name means 'high tree' and refers to a tall redwood, first mentioned in 1774 by Palou. Tradition connects the name with the "twin redwoods," one of them still standing on the creek near the station. The name was applied by Leland Stanford to his estate and in 1891 by the Southern Pacific to the station at Stanford University. The word *palo* is also used in Palo Verde (green tree), Palo Cedro (cedar tree), Dos Palos (two trees), Palo Colorado (redwood).

Palomar Mountain [San Diego]. The name, 'place of the pigeons,' was used in Mexican times and revived in 1901 after the mountain had been called Smith Mountain for many years.

Palo Verde. The name of the green-barked tree, found native in dry regions of southern California, was often used in Spanish times as a place name and is preserved in Imperial County. In some places [Stanislaus and Los Angeles counties] the name may refer simply to a 'green tree.'

Pamo Valley [San Diego]. An Indian rancheria called *Pamo* was mentioned in 1778. In 1843 the name was applied to a land grant.

Panamint, pan'-a-mint [Inyo]. The name is derived from a division of Shoshonean Indians who formerly occupied the region, possibly the *Beñemes* mentioned in 1776. The present spelling is recorded in 1861.

Panoche [San Benito, Fresno]. A place called *Panocha* was recorded July 4, 1840. The name is found in a land grant, *Panocha de San Juan* [Merced]; a land claim, *Panoche Grande* [San Benito]; and on the map of another grant [Santa Barbara]. *Panoche* was a kind of sweet substance which Indians obtained from a reed.

Paoha Island [Mono Lake]. The name was applied by the Geological Survey in 1882. *Paoha* is the Mono Indian word for 'water babies,' naked female spirits.

Paraiso, pa-ry'-zoh [Monterey]. The name means 'paradise' and is the only survivor of several places so named.

Pardee Lake [Amador, Calaveras]. The reservoir was named for George C. Pardee, governor of California, 1903–1907.

Parker Dam [San Bernardino]. Named after the station in Arizona, which in turn had been named in 1906 for Earl H. Parker, location engineer of the Santa Fe.

Pasadena, pas-a-dee′-na [Los Angeles]. The melodious name, adopted by the stockholders of the Indiana Colony in 1875, was taken from the language of the Chippewa Indians of the Mississippi Valley and means 'valley.'

Paskenta [Tehama]. Derived from the Central Wintun Indian word *paskenti* (under the bank).

Paso Robles, pa′-so roh′-b'ls [San Luis Obispo]. The city was founded in 1886 with the name El Paso de Robles (pass of oaks). The wealth of deciduous oaks in the vicinity was mentioned by the Anza expedition in 1776. In 1844 the name Paso de Robles was applied to a land grant.

Patterson [Stanislaus]. Named in 1910 for John D. Patterson, who had purchased the land in 1864.

Patterson Pass [Alameda]. So named because A. J. Patterson's wagon turned over here in a heavy storm in the 1850's.

Patton [San Bernardino]. The Santa Fe station was named in 1895 for Henry Patton, of Santa Barbara.

Pauma [San Diego]. The name of a rancheria of Luiseño Indians, recorded in the 1790's; applied to a grant in 1844.

Peanut [Trinity]. So named in 1900 by the postmaster of Weaverville because the name was unique and because he was fond of peanuts.

Pedernales Point, ped-er-nal′-es [Santa Barbara]. In August, 1769, Portolá's soldiers called a near-by rancheria *Los Pedernales* because they had gathered *pedernales* (flints) there. The name was first attached to Rocky Point.

Penitencia Creek [Santa Clara]. *Arroyo de la Penitencia* (creek of penitence) was recorded in the early 1840's, perhaps named for an adobe house serving as a confessional.

Penryn [Placer]. The name of the city in Wales (Penrhyn) was given to the railroad station in the 1870's.

Perris [Riverside]. Named in 1886 for Fred T. Perris, chief engineer for the California Southern R.R.

Pescadero, pes-ka-dehr′-oh. The name, 'fishing place' in maritime Spanish, used often in California, was applied in five land grants, and survives in Santa Clara, San Mateo, Monterey, and San Joaquin counties.

Petaluma, pet-a-loo'-ma [Sonoma]. Named for a division of the Miwok Indians. *El llano* (plain) *de los Petalumas* is mentioned in 1819. The word is said to mean 'flat back.' It was applied to a land grant in 1834, and to the city in 1851.

Pfeiffer, py'-fer [Monterey]. The name of Michael Pfeiffer, an early settler, was applied to the point in the 1880's and to the state park in 1933.

Picacho, pi-kah'-choh. The Spanish word for 'peak' has survived in several places; the most notable is Picacho Peak (literally 'peak peak') in Imperial County.

Pico, pee'-koh. The name of several Mexican families is preserved in a number of features. Pico in Los Angeles County was named for Pio Pico, the last Mexican governor. Pico Canyon in that county preserves the name of Andrés Pico, pioneer of coal-oil manufacturing in the state.

Pico Blanco [Monterey]. The descriptive name, 'white peak,' was probably applied in Spanish times.

Piedmont [Alameda]. Probably a transfer name, although the community is actually at the 'foot of the mountain.'

Piedra, pee-ay'-dra. The Spanish name for 'rock' is still found in several places, such as Point Piedras Blancas (white rocks point) and Piedra Azul Creek (blue rock creek).

Pigeon Point [San Mateo]. Applied in 1858 by the Coast Survey because the clipper ship *Carrier Pigeon* had been wrecked here, on May 6, 1853.

Pilarcitos, pil-ar-see'-tos [San Mateo]. The 'little pillar-like rocks' are probably those in the formation south of Pillar Point. Applied to a land grant in 1836.

Pillar Point [San Mateo]. A place was called *El Pilar* in 1796, probably for the rocky formation. Applied to the point in 1862.

Pinchot, Mount [Fresno]. Named by J. N. LeConte, for Gifford Pinchot, then Chief of the Division of Forestry.

Pinnacles National Monument. The jagged formations in San Benito County, discovered by Vancouver in 1794, were proclaimed a national monument in 1908.

Pinole, pi-nohl' [Contra Costa]. The Mexican word *pinole* for a meal made of grain or seed was used as early as 1775 by Spaniards in telling of a food made by the Indians in the district. It was given to a land grant in 1823.

Pinos, py'-nos, pee'-nos. The Spanish word for 'pines' is found in Point Pinos, Los Pinos Peak, Tres Pinos Creek.

Pinto. The word means 'mottled' in the Southwest and is applied to piebald horses, as well as to mountains and rocks which show veins of various colors.

Pinyon. The Spanish word *piñón*, designating the pine-nut seed, valued by the Indians as food, is found in a number of peaks, valleys, and creeks.

Piru, pi-roo' [Ventura]. Apparently an Indian name of Shoshonean origin, recorded in 1817.

Pisgah, Mount [San Bernardino]. A crater named after the peak in Palestine from which Moses saw the promised land.

Pismo [San Luis Obispo]. A Chumash Indian name (*pismo* probably means 'tar') applied to a land grant in 1840.

Pit River. Named by the Hudson's Bay trappers in the 1820's because the Indians on its banks dug pits to trap animals. Until recent times often spelled Pitt and associated with the English statesman.

Pittsburg [Contra Costa]. Founded as New York of the Pacific in 1849 by Colonel J. D. Stevenson and Dr. W. C. Parker of the N. Y. Volunteers of 1847. At the time of the Mount Diablo coal boom in the 1860's the name Pittsburg was given to present Pittsburg Landing. In 1911 old New York was renamed Pittsburg.

Piute. Loosely applied to several language groups of Indians living along the Nevada boundary. As a place name, sometimes spelled Paiute and Pahute, it is found from Lassen to San Bernardino counties. The older form, Pahute, indicates that the name means 'water Utes.'

Placentia, pla-sent'-cha [Orange]. The name was given to the school district in 1884, possibly after the town in Newfoundland, and transferred to the town in 1910.

Placer, plass'-er. A Western term of Spanish origin for deposits containing gold particles obtainable by washing.

Placerville [El Dorado], named in 1850, and Placer County, created in 1851, were named because of the presence of rich placers. *See* Hangtown Creek.

Playa. The Spanish term for 'beach' and 'dry lake bed' was frequently used in Spanish and Mexican times and is now popular for resorts and subdivisions. Pronunciation varies according to locality: ply'-yah, ply'-ah, play'-a.

Pleasanton [Alameda]. Named in 1867 for General Alfred Pleasonton, an often-cited officer in the Mexican and Civil wars. The name has been misspelled since the 1870's.

Plumas County. Created in 1854 and so named because the county is drained by the Feather River, called *Rio de las Plumas* in Mexican times.

Pomona [Los Angeles]. The name of the Roman goddess of orchards was given to the city in 1875.

Ponderosa Way. A 200-mile firebreak in the Sierra foothills to protect the higher ponderosa pine country.

Porterville [Tulare]. In 1864 R. Porter Putnam laid out the town and named it for himself.

Portola, por-toh'-la. Gaspar de Portolá, leader of the expedition of 1769, a detachment of which discovered San Francisco Bay, is honored in two small places in Plumas and San Mateo counties and in the State Park [San Mateo].

Potrero. The word for 'pasture' is frequent in central and southern counties, especially in San Diego. Most of the names go back to Spanish times.

Poway, pow'-way, pow'-wye [San Diego]. Apparently derived from Paguay, mentioned as a rancho in 1828, a land grant in 1839, and an arroyo in 1841.

Powell, Mount [Inyo]. Named in 1912 by the Geological Survey, in memory of John W. Powell, who navigated the Colorado through the Grand Canyon in 1869.

Pozo, Posita. The word for 'well' or 'water hole' (*poso* or *pozo*) and its diminutive form were often used in Spanish times, especially on maps of land grants, and have survived in Alameda, Los Angeles, Kern, San Luis Obispo, and Santa Barbara counties. **Posey** [Tulare] is a rural American pronunciation of the same word.

Project City. *See* Central Valley.

Providence Mountains [San Bernardino]. The name appeared on maps in 1857, originally for the entire mountain chain. Probably so named by early travelers who found springs here.

Pudding Creek [Mendocino]. In local tradition, the sailors called the anchorage at Noyo River "Put In Creek," and landlubbers later transferred the name to the stream north of Fort Bragg and changed the spelling.

Puente, poo-en′-te, pwen′-te [Los Angeles]. A *Llano de la Puente* (plain of the bridge) was mentioned by Portolá in 1770. On July 30, 1769, the expedition built a bridge of poles in order to cross an arroyo. In 1842 the name was applied to the Puente de San Gabriel land grant.

Puerto. There were many *puertos* (ports, bays) along the coast in Spanish times, but none of these names have survived. The term was used inland for 'pass,' or 'defile'; Puerto Creek [Stanislaus] preserves the land-grant name (1844).

Pulgas. The frequent occurrence of the word for 'fleas' since the Portolá expedition of 1769 shows that the Spaniards were just as annoyed by the little insects as the Americans. The word survives as a place name in several counties.

Punta. In Spanish times the less important capes along the coast were called *puntas* (points). The term has survived in Punta Gorda, Punta de Pinos, Punta del Castillo, Punta de los Muertos.

Purisima, pur-iss′-i-ma. The name is an abbreviation of La Purísima Concepción (the Immaculate Conception). Purisima Point [Santa Barbara] was named for the near-by mission, founded in 1787. The name is also applied to a creek and a settlement in San Mateo County.

Putah Creek, poo′-ta, pew′-ta [Napa, Solano]. The stream preserves the name of a branch of the Patwin Indians who once dwelt on its banks. Its similarity to Spanish *puta,* 'harlot,' is purely accidental.

Pywiack Cascade [Yosemite N. P.]. The Indian name was recorded by John Muir in 1873. *Py-we-ack* was the natives' name for Tenaya Lake.

Quicksilver. The places in Los Angeles and Sonoma counties are reminiscent of quicksilver booms, which with few exceptions petered out. *See* Almaden.

Quinado Canyon [Monterey]. Derived from an Indian word for 'evil smelling,' referring here to the sulphur springs.

Quincy. When the town became the seat of Plumas County in 1854, it was named after Quincy, Illinois, the home town of the owner of the hotel.

Ramona [San Diego]. The name was given to this community (and several others) in the late 1880's when Helen Hunt Jackson's novel was at the height of its popularity.

Rancho Cordova [Sacramento]. Named in 1955 after the Cordova Vineyards on the Rancho de los Americanos grant.

Rancho Santa Fe [San Diego]. In 1906 the Santa Fe developed the San Dieguito Rancho as an experimental station for growing eucalyptus trees; in 1927 the ranch was sold for subdivision but the name Santa Fe was retained.

Randsburg [Kern]. Applied as a good omen in 1895, after the Rand, the ridge near Johannesburg, Transvaal, since 1886 one of the world's richest gold-mining districts.

Reading Peak, red-ing [Lassen N. P.]. Pierson B. Reading, pioneer of the upper Sacramento Valley, discovered gold in the Trinity region in 1848.

Red Bluff [Tehama]. Founded in 1850 and named after the fifty-foot reddish bluff on the Sacramento River.

Redding [Shasta]. The name of B. B. Redding, land agent of the Central Pacific, was given to the station in 1872. From 1874 to 1880 the name was Reading (pron. red-ding) in honor of Pierson B. Reading, pioneer of 1843.

Redlands [San Bernardino]. The town was so named in 1887 because of the reddish soil.

Redondo Beach [Los Angeles]. Founded in 1881 and apparently named after the adjoining Rancho Sausal Redondo (round willow grove).

Redwood. The popular name for the coast Sequoia is found in many places where the mighty tree grows or once grew. Redwood Empire is the common designation of the regions traversed by the Redwood Highway. In some places the name may be a translation of the Spanish *palo colorado*.

Reedley [Fresno]. In 1888 Thomas L. Reed, a veteran of Sherman's march to the sea, gave half of his holdings to the city but declined the honor of having his name applied to the place, whereupon the suffix *-ley* was added.

Refugio Pass [Santa Barbara]. The name appears in the land grant *Nuestra Señora del Refugio* (Our Lady of the Refuge) of 1794, and is repeatedly recorded in later years in the abbreviated form.

Requa [Del Norte]. Derived from the Yurok Indian *re'kwoi* (creek mouth), recorded as Rechwa in 1851.

Reyes, Point, rays [Marin]. The name *Punta de los Reyes* was applied by the Vizcaíno expedition, which reached the point on January 6, 1603, the day of the 'three holy kings.' The hybrid form has appeared on maps since 1841.

Rheem [Contra Costa]. Named for Donald L. Rheem, who started the development in 1944.

Rialto [San Bernardino]. Named in 1887. Rialto is a short form of Rivus Altus, the name of the Grand Canal of Venice.

Ricardo [Kern]. Named in 1898 for the Indian who kept the inn at the old stage stop.

Richardson Bay [Marin]. Named for William A. Richardson, who erected the first building in the city of San Francisco in 1835 and soon after became captain of the port of San Francisco and grantee of Sausalito Rancho.

Richmond [Contra Costa]. Probably a transfer name from the East, applied to the point by the Coast Survey in 1852. The city was named after the point in 1905.

Rio, ree'-oh. The word for 'river' is preserved as a generic term in Rio Hondo [Los Angeles]. It has been frequently used in American times for towns: Rio Oso, El Rio, Dos Rios, Rio Linda, Rio Nido, Rio Vista.

Ripon [San Joaquin]. Named in 1876 after the postmaster's home town in Wisconsin.

Ritter, Mount [Madera]. Named by the Whitney Survey in 1864 for Karl Ritter, famous German geographer.

Riverside. The city was named in 1871 because of its location on the banks of a channel of the Santa Ana River. The county was named after the city in 1893.

Roble, Roblar. The words for 'deciduous oak' and 'oak grove' survive in several place names. *See* Paso Robles.

Rockaway Beach [San Mateo]. Named after Rockaway, Long Island. The name means 'sandy land' in Delaware Indian.

Rodeo, roh-day′-oh. The word for 'roundup' has become a part of California speech and is found in many place names, most important of which is the town [Contra Costa].

Rohnerville [Humboldt]. Henry Rohner, a Swiss pioneer of 1849, opened a store here in 1859.

Rosecrans, Fort [San Diego]. Named by the War Department in 1899, in memory of W. S. Rosecrans, commander of the Army of the Cumberland, 1862–1863, who died in 1898.

Roseville [Placer]. The popular American place name was given to the Central Pacific station in 1864.

Ross [Marin]. James Ross settled here in 1859.

Rough and Ready [Nevada]. A mining camp of gold-rush days, the only survivor of several places bearing the nickname of General (later President) Zachary Taylor.

Royce, Mount [Fresno]. Named in 1929 for Josiah Royce, American philosopher, a native of Grass Valley.

Rubicon River [El Dorado]. The river was called "The Rubicon" in 1873, probably in jesting analogy to Caesar's crossing of the Rubicon.

Rubidoux, Mount [Riverside]. Named for Louis Robidoux, pioneer of 1844 and one-time owner of Rancho Jurupa.

Russian River [Sonoma]. The Russians, who occupied the territory between Bodega Bay and Fort Ross from 1812 to 1841, called the river *Slavianka*. The Spanish called it *San Ignacio* and also *Rio Ruso*. The present name came into use after the American occupation.

Sacramento, sack-ra-men′-toh. The Spanish name, 'Holy Sacrament,' was applied to the Feather River in 1808; it was later assumed that the lower Sacramento was the same stream. In 1817 the two main rivers of the valley were recorded as Sacramento and San Joaquin rivers, but the course of the former was not identified with the name until the 1830's. The city was laid out in 1848–1849 and named after the river by John A. Sutter, Jr., and Sam Brannan. The county, one of the original twenty-seven, was named in 1850.

Saint George [Del Norte].The point was named by Vancouver on April 23, 1792, the day of England's patron saint.

Saint Helena, Mount [Lake, Napa]. The name of the mountain was first recorded as Mount St. Helena in 1851, but also appeared on American maps as Mount Helen until the late 1860's. None of the romantic stories concerning the naming of the mountain by the Russians has been substantiated. The town was named in 1855 for the St. Helena Division of the Sons of Temperance, which in turn had been named for the mountain.

Sal, Point [Santa Barbara]. Named in 1792 by Vancouver for Hermenegildo Sal, *comandante* at San Francisco.

Salada Beach, sa-lah'-da [San Mateo]. Named in 1905 after near-by Laguna Salada (salty lagoon).

Salida, sa-ly'-da [Stanislaus]. The word meaning 'departure' in Spanish was applied to the station in 1870.

Salinas, sa-lee'-nas [Monterey]. The origin of the name is found in the *salinas* (salt marshes) near the mouth of the river. The name was used for a land grant before 1795, but it was not in general use for the river until 1846. The name of the city is recorded in 1860.

Salsipuedes, sal-see-poo-eh'-des. The phrase, meaning 'get out [of a tight place] if you can,' was a popular place name in Spanish times. It is preserved in the names in Monterey, San Luis Obispo, and Santa Barbara counties.

Salton Sea [Riverside]. In 1892 the lake bed was named after the Southern Pacific station on its shore. The name, probably from 'salt,' was kept for the lake that formed in 1907.

San Andreas, an-dray'-as [San Mateo]. The valley was named San Andrés by Palou on November 30, 1774, feast day of Saint Andrew, the apostle. **San Andreas** [Calaveras]. The camp was settled and named by Mexican miners in 1848.

San Anselmo, an-sel'-mo [Marin]. *Cañada de Anselmo* appears in the papers of the *Punta de Quintin* grant of 1840, and was applied in the present form to the North Pacific Coast R.R. station in the 1890's. The *cañada* (valley) was very likely named for a baptized Indian, and the *San* was added to the name later.

San Antonio. The name of the holy Anthony of Padua was one of the favorite saints' names given to places in Spanish times. The mission and river in Monterey County and some twenty land grants and claims bear the name. Of the still existing names those in Monterey and San Bernardino counties were recorded as early as the 1770's.

San Ardo [Monterey]. This is not a saint's name but an abbreviation of San Bernardo, applied in 1886 to avoid confusion with San Bernardino.

San Benito. The valley was named in 1772 for Saint Benedict, founder of the Benedictine Order, and soon afterward the name was applied to the river. In 1842 it was given to a land grant and in 1874 to the county.

San Bernardino. The name of the Italian saint of the 15th century was recorded as a place name in 1810. In 1842 it was applied to a land grant, on a part of which Mormons in 1851 started a settlement, the nucleus for the present city. The mountains are mentioned before 1850, the county was named in 1853, and the national forest in 1893. The name also occurred in other parts of the state.

San Bruno [San Mateo]. The name of the German saint of the 11th century was apparently first given to a creek by Palou in 1774. *Sierra de San Bruno* (San Bruno Mountains) was recorded in 1826, and San Bruno House, the nucleus of the town, existed in 1862.

San Buenaventura [Ventura]. The mission was founded in 1782 and named for a 13th-century saint. The name (with and without the "San") was also applied, in the 1820's, to a mythical river flowing from the Rocky Mountains to the Pacific, but here it simply meant 'good fortune river.'

San Carlos, kar'-los. The mission in Monterey County was named in 1770 for Saint Charles Borromeo, a leader of the

Counterreformation in the 16th century. The pass in Riverside County was named by Anza in 1774 when he led
the first party across the mountains into California. The
city [San Mateo] was so named in 1887 because it was believed that Portolá's men saw San Francisco Bay from the
hills on Saint Charles' day, November 4, 1769.

San Clemente Island, kle-men'-te [Los Angeles]. Named by
Vizcaíno about November 25, 1602, in honor of Saint Clem-
ent, whose feast day is the 23d of November. The town
in Orange County was named in 1925 after the island.

San Diego. The bay was named by Vizcaíno in 1602, in honor
of Saint Didacus of Alcalá, a Franciscan saint of the 15th
century. The mission was named in 1769, the county in
1850, and the new city in 1856.

San Dieguito Valley [San Diego]. The Spanish name of Saint
James the Less, one of the Twelve Apostles. The arroyo
[San Dieguito River] and the site of *San Dieguillo* were
mentioned by Font on January 10, 1776. A rancheria named
San Dieguito was mentioned in 1778, and the name was
applied to a land grant in the early 1840's.

San Dimas, dee'-mas [Los Angeles]. The town was laid out
in 1886 and named after the canyon, which had been
named in Spanish times for the penitent robber, crucified
at the right side of Christ.

San Elijo Lagoon [San Diego]. A camping place of the Portolá
expedition was called San Alejo on July 16, 1769, obviously
for Saint Alexius, whose feast day is July 17. Later, the
name shifted southward and was applied to the lagoon.

San Emigdio [Kern]. The Spanish name of Saint Emygdius,
a German saint of the 4th century, was applied to a rancho
and station of Santa Barbara Mission before 1824, and
continued to be used in the land grant of 1842.

San Felipe. Places in San Diego, San Benito, and Santa Clara
counties honor one of the saints named Philip.

San Fernando [Los Angeles]. The mission established in 1797
honored Saint Ferdinand, King of Castile and Leon in the
13th century. Pass, range, river are mentioned in the early
1850's; the city was named in 1874.

San Francisco. *Bahia de San Francisco* was the name given in honor of Saint Francis of Assisi to what is now Drakes Bay, on November 7, 1595. For 174 years the name remained a vague geographical conception until a detachment of the Portolá expedition, searching for Monterey Bay, beheld the large body of water between them and Point Reyes, from the hills near Point San Pedro on October 31, 1769. They thought that they were looking upon the original bay or port of San Francisco. A few days later, when they saw what is now known as San Francisco Bay, they called it the "estuary of the port of San Francisco." The presidio and the mission, *La Mision de . . . San Francisco de Asis* (now popularly known as Mission Dolores), were established in 1776. The town of Yerba Buena was renamed San Francisco in 1847, and the county, one of the original twenty-seven, was created and named in 1850.

San Francisquito Creek, fran-sis-kee′-toh [Santa Clara]. The place was dedicated to Saint Francis by Palou in 1774 as a suitable site for a mission. The stream was mentioned as the *Arroyo de San Francisco* by Anza in 1776. When the mission was established farther north (now Mission Dolores) the creek became known as *Arroyo de San Francisquito* (little San Francisco Creek). The canyon [Los Angeles] bears the land-grant name of 1845.

San Gabriel [Los Angeles]. Named for the Archangel Gabriel in 1771. The river was known by this name before 1782; the mountain range as early as 1806.

Sanger [Fresno]. Named in 1888 by the Southern Pacific, for Joseph Sanger, Jr., an official of the railroad.

San Geronimo, je-ron′-i-mo [Marin]. The Spanish name of Saint Jerome was given to a land grant in 1844. In 1875 it was applied to the station of the North Pacific Coast R.R.

San Gorgonio, gor-gohn′-yoh [Riverside, San Bernardino]. The name of a Christian martyr of the 4th century was given to a cattle ranch of the San Gabriel Mission before 1824. In 1843 a land grant was named San Jacinto y San Gorgonio. The pass and the mountains have been known by the name since the early 1850's.

San Gregorio [San Mateo]. The name of Saint Gregory was given to a land grant of 1839, and was applied to the post office in the 1860's.

Sanhedrin, Mount [Mendocino]. The name is recorded in 1874. The region was settled by Missourians, who transferred the name Sanhedrin from their home state. The Missouri mountain was probably named for the supreme council of the Jews.

San Jacinto, ja-sin'-toh, a-sin'-toh [Riverside]. *San Jacinto Viejo* was a cattle ranch of Mission San Luis Rey in 1821. In the 1840's the name San Jacinto (Saint Hyacinth) was applied to three land grants, and in 1872 to the town.

San Joaquin, wah-keen'. The name of Saint Joachim, father of the Virgin Mary, was applied to the river by Gabriel Moraga in 1806 or earlier. The county was named after the river in 1850. The name was also used for several land grants in other parts of the state and has been preserved in several minor features.

San Jose, san-o-zay' [Santa Clara]. The *pueblo,* the first in Upper California, was founded in 1777 and named for Saint Joseph, husband of the Virgin Mary. San José is perhaps the most popular saint's name in Spanish-speaking countries. *See* Mission San Jose.

San Juan Bautista, san wahn baw-tis'-ta [San Benito]. The mission was named in 1797 for Saint John the Baptist. The post office was called San Juan in 1852 but this name was later changed to the complete form.

San Juan Capistrano, san wahn kap-i-strah'-noh [Orange]. The mission was named in 1776 in honor of Saint John Capistran, the fighting priest of the 15th century who took a heroic part in the defense of Vienna against the Turks. The name of the post office was originally Capistrano.

San Leandro [Alameda]. A land grant of 1839 was named after *Arroyo de San Leandro* (Creek of Saint Leander) mentioned in 1828. The town was laid out and named in 1855.

San Lorenzo [Alameda]. The two 'Saint Lawrence' land grants (1841, 1842) were apparently named after the *Arroyo de San Lorenzo* (now San Lorenzo Creek). The town was named before 1854. **San Lorenzo River** [Santa Cruz] was named by the Portolá expedition October 17, 1769.

San Lucas [Monterey]. Founded in 1886 and named after the San Lucas Rancho, granted in 1842, and named for Saint Luke.

San Luis Creek [Merced]. *San Luis Gonzaga* (for a Jesuit of the 16th century) was mentioned in 1806. This name was used for titles of land grants in 1834 and 1841.

San Luis Obispo. The mission was established in 1772, and named for Louis, Bishop of Toulouse, a 13th-century saint. City and county were named after the mission in 1850.

San Luis Rey [San Diego]. Derived from the mission established in 1798 and named for Saint Louis, King of France.

San Marcos [San Diego]. *El Valle S. Marcos* (Saint Mark's valley) was mentioned in 1797 and used for a land grant, *Vallecitos de San Marcos,* in 1840; it was applied to the station in 1887. **San Marcos Pass** [Santa Barbara], recorded in 1854, was probably named after the San Marcos land grant of 1846. A mission rancho by that name was mentioned in 1817.

San Marino, ma-ree'-noh [Los Angeles]. James de Barth Shorb built a home here in 1878 and named it San Marino after his home in Maryland. When Henry E. Huntington bought the place in 1903 he retained the name.

San Martin [Santa Clara]. Named by Martin Murphy, immigrant of 1844, for his patron saint.

San Martin, Cape [Monterey]. The name was given to the cape by the Coast Survey in 1870; it was in the latitude of Cape San Martin, mentioned by Cabrillo in 1542.

San Mateo, ma-tay'-oh. *Arroyo de San Matheo* is recorded in 1776. In the 1790's the Mission Dolores established a sheep ranch there, and in 1840 and 1846 the name was applied to land grants. The county was named in 1856 and the railroad station in 1863. **San Mateo Canyon** [San Diego]. *Arroyo de San Mateo* was mentioned in 1778. Both names honor the evangelist and apostle, Saint Matthew.

San Miguel Island, mi-gel'. The name of Saint Michael was first bestowed upon what is now Santa Rosa Island. Since

the early 1790's the name has been identified with the present place. **San Miguel** [San Luis Obispo]. The railroad
station was named in 1886 after the mission, which had
been named in 1797 for the Archangel Michael.

San Nicolas Island [Santa Barbara]. Named by the Vizcaíno
expedition, probably on December 6, 1602, the feast day
of Saint Nicholas, the saint of Myra (4th century).

San Onofre, o'-no-fre [San Diego]. The name of the Egyptian
hermit, Saint Onuphrius, was mentioned for a mission
rancho in 1828, and was applied to a land grant in 1836.

San Pablo. In 1811, or earlier, the point in Contra Costa
County was named for Saint Paul, and the point opposite
in Marin County was named San Pedro for Saint Peter.
In 1823 the name San Pablo was used for two provisional
land grants, and in the 1850's the name was applied to the
bay by the Coast Survey.

San Pasqual, pa-skwal' [San Diego]. Mentioned after 1800
as a rancheria under the jurisdiction of San Diego; organized as a *pueblo* in 1835. The name (sometimes spelled Pas-
cual) is from Saint Pascal Baylon, a 16th-century Spanish
saint. It gained historical significance when the American
forces under Kearny and the Mexicans under Andrés Pico
fought the "battle of San Pasqual," as the skirmish of
December 6, 1846, is usually called.

San Pedro, pee'-droh, pay'-droh. Saint Peter, the name of
several holy men, was a favorite for place names in Spanish
times and has survived in a number of geographical features. The bay in Los Angeles County was named by members of the Vizcaíno expedition in 1602, probably for the
Bishop of Alexandria. The name was given to land grants
before 1799 and in 1822. It has been used for the harbor
since the 1840's and for the city since 1854. The names in
San Mateo County go back to a rancho of Mission Dolores
recorded in 1791, and to the land grant of 1839. The point
in Marin County was probably named after an Indian
rancheria named San Pedro by Spaniards, recorded in 1807.

San Quentin [Marin]. The point and the penitentiary were
not named in honor of the saint but only for his namesake,

a notorious Indian renegade, Quintin, who was captured here in 1824. The "San" was added by Americans later.

San Rafael, ra-fell' [Marin]. The mission was founded in 1817, and named *La Mision de San Rafael Arcangel,* for the guardian archangel of humanity. In 1851 the post office was named after the mission. The San Rafael Mountains in Santa Barbara and Ventura counties and some minor features were probably also named for the archangel.

San Ramon, ra-mohn' [Contra Costa]. The creek was named in the 1830's for a caretaker of Mission San Jose; the "San" was added for good measure. Later, several land grants were named after the creek.

San Simeon [San Luis Obispo]. *San Simeon* as the name of a rancho of Mission San Miguel was recorded in 1819 and again in 1827. The name honors Saint Simon, whose feast day is February 18. An *Arroyo de San Simon* is shown on a map of 1841; in 1842 the name was given to a land grant, and in 1874 to the post office.

Santa Ana [Orange]. The river was named by the soldiers of the Portolá expedition on July 28, 1769. The feast day of Saint Anne, mother of the Virgin Mary, had been celebrated on the 26th. After 1810 the name appeared repeatedly in mission records. Several land grants were named after the river. In 1847 the name is recorded for a settlement; the modern city was founded and named in 1869. The name is also preserved in a creek, a valley, and a mountain in San Benito County, and in a creek in Ventura County.

Santa Anita, a-nee'-ta [Los Angeles]. The Santa Anita land grant of 1841 was purchased and developed by E. J. ("Lucky") Baldwin in 1875.

Santa Barbara. *La Canal de Santa Barbara* was the name applied to Santa Barbara Channel by Vizcaíno on December 4, 1602, the day of the Roman maiden who was beheaded by her father because she had become a Christian. At the same time the name was apparently also given to the easternmost of the Anacapa Islands but was later transferred to the present Santa Barbara Island. The name

Santa Barbara Virgen y Martyr was applied to the presidio in 1782 and to the mission in 1786. City and county were named in 1850.

Santa Catalina Island, kat-a-lee'-na. Named by Vizcaíno on November 25, 1602, feast day of the holy Catherine of Alexandria. In 1846 the island was made a grant.

Santa Clara. The mission, established in 1777, was named for the founder of the Franciscan order of Poor Clares, and the town was later named for the mission. The county, one of the original twenty-seven, was named in 1850, and the name for the valley became current in the early 1850's. **Santa Clara River** [Los Angeles, Ventura]. The valley was named for the same saint by the Portolá expedition in 1769; the name was soon applied to the river, and in 1837 to a land grant.

Santa Cruz. A creek near the present city, probably Major's Mill Creek, was named *Arroyo de Santa Cruz* (Holy Cross Creek) by the Portolá expedition in 1769. In 1791 *La Mision de la Exaltacion de la Santa Cruz* was established. In 1797 a settlement was founded near the mission and was called *Villa de Branciforte,* a name that was subsequently changed to Santa Cruz. Santa Cruz Mountains are recorded since 1838. The county was named in 1851. **Santa Cruz Island.** The name was given in 1769 to one of the channel islands on which an Indian found a cross lost by a padre. Since 1770 the name has been identified with the present Santa Cruz Island. The name Santa Cruz is also found in Mariposa, Santa Barbara, and other counties.

Santa Lucia Range, loo-see'-a, -shee'-a. The name was given to the mountains by Vizcaíno about December 14, 1602, in honor of Saint Lucy, whose day is December 13.

Santa Margarita [San Diego]. The valley was named by the Portolá expedition on July 20, 1769, because it was the day of holy Margaret of Antioch. In 1836 the name was used for a land grant and later for the river and the mountains.

Santa Margarita [San Luis Obispo]. The name is mentioned by Anza in 1776. It was apparently applied before 1790 to a place where San Luis Obispo Mission raised hogs and later to an *asistencia*. The name honors the holy Margaret of Cortona.

Santa Maria, ma-ree'-a. The name of the mother of Jesus was used for place names in Spanish and Mexican times in the form of *Nuestra Señora de* (Our Lady of) followed by a name such as Guadalupe or Refugio; the name Santa Maria very often honors other saints named Mary. The name of the valley in San Diego County was given to a land grant, *Valle de Pamo* or *Santa Maria,* in 1843. The name in Santa Barbara County was recorded for Purisima Point in 1782; for a land grant, *Tepusquet* or *Santa Maria,* in 1837; and in 1882 it was applied to the railroad station.

Santa Monica, mon'-i-ka [Los Angeles]. The name may have been applied by the second Portolá expedition on May 4, 1770, the day of holy Monica, mother of Saint Augustine. It appears in 1839 in the land grant San Vicente y Santa Monica, on which the modern city was founded in the early 1870's. *Sierra de Santa Monica* was recorded in 1822.

Santa Paula, paul'-a [Ventura]. The city was laid out and named in 1872 on the Rancho Santa Paula y Saticoy, granted in 1834 and 1840. A stock ranch of Mission San Buenaventura, named for Saint Paula, a noble Roman matron, a disciple of Saint Jerome, is recorded in 1834.

Santa Rita. The name (an abbreviation of Santa Margarita) in Merced County was mentioned as early as 1806 and was used in the land grant *Sanjon de Santa Rita* in 1841. The name in Monterey County goes back to the grant *Los Gatos* or *Santa Rita* of 1824; the names in Alameda and Santa Barbara counties were likewise from land grants.

Santa Rosa. A very popular name in Spanish times, probably because Santa Rosa de Lima (Saint Rose of Lima) was for a long time the only female saint of America. *Isla de Santa Rosa* was apparently the name given in 1774 to San Miguel Island, but since the 1790's the name has been identified with the island which is now so called. The city in Sonoma County was named in 1853; the name had been used for land grants in 1831 and 1841, and for the creek in 1833. The names of the mountains in San Diego and Riverside, the creek in San Luis Obispo, and the hills and the creek in Santa Barbara counties were likewise transmitted through land grants named Santa Rosa. In the last-named county the name dates from August 30, 1769, when the Portolá expedition gave Santa Rosa as an alternate name for what is now the Santa Ynez River.

Santa Susana [Ventura]. A place so named was mentioned in 1804, and a grade bore the name in 1834. The name was given for a saint of the 3d century. The mountains were mentioned with this name in 1850.

Santa Ynez, ee-nez' [Santa Barbara]. The mission *Santa Ines, Virgen y Martir* was founded in 1804; the river and mountains were named after it. The town was named in 1882.

Santa Ysabel [San Diego]. The name probably honoring Saint Elizabeth, Queen of Portugal, was mentioned in 1818; in 1821 Mission San Diego established an *asistencia* there. In 1844 the name was applied to a land grant, and in 1875 to the Indian Reservation.

Santiago [Orange]. The name of Santiago (Saint James), patron saint of Spain, whose feast day is July 25, was given to the tributary of the Santa Ana River by the Portolá expedition on July 27, 1769. In 1810 and 1846 the name was used for land grants.

San Vicente. A mountain in Los Angeles, a valley in Monterey, creeks in San Diego, Santa Cruz, and San Mateo counties are named for one of the many holy Vincents. All these names were preserved through land grants.

San Ysidro, ee-see'-droh [San Diego]. The name of Saint Isidore, of the 7th century, given to the mountain and an Indian rancheria in Spanish times, was applied to the town in 1909.

Saranap [Contra Costa]. The name was coined in 1913 from *Sara Nap*thaly.

Saratoga [Santa Clara]. The post office was so named in 1867 because the waters of near-by Pacific Congress Springs resemble those of Saratoga Springs in New York.

Saticoy [Ventura]. Derived from what is probably a Chumash Indian village, mentioned with the present spelling, in a letter of May 20, 1826. It is found in the Santa Paula y Saticoy land grant of 1834, and was applied to the town in 1861.

Saugus [Los Angeles]. A transfer name from Massachusetts, the original meaning of which is 'outlet' or 'mouth' in the Algonkian Indian dialects. The station was named in 1879.

Sausalito, saw-sa-lee'-to [Marin]. *Sausalito* means 'little willow grove.' The name was recorded as early as 1831. The misspelling Saucelito occurred in the 1850's, was transferred to the new town in 1868, and persisted sporadically until after 1900.

Schonchin Butte, scon'-shin [Lava Beds N. M.]. The name commemorates the old chief of the Modocs who signed a treaty in 1864 and, as the story goes, pointed to the mountain as a witness to his pledge.

Scotia [Humboldt]. Named in 1885 by a number of families from Nova Scotia.

Scott River [Siskiyou]. The river as well as the mountains and the valley commemorate John W. Scott, who discovered gold here in 1850.

Scotty's Castle [Death Valley]. Walter ("Death Valley") Scott, formerly with Buffalo Bill's Wild West Show, started building the enormous structure on the old Staininger Ranch in 1923.

Searles Lake [San Bernardino]. The brothers John and Dennis Searles discovered borax in the dry lake in 1863.

Sebastopol, se-bas'-to-pol [Sonoma]. The town is the sole survivor of four Sebastopols, all named in 1854 when the siege of the Russian seaport by the British and French caused great excitement throughout the world. The immediate cause for the naming is said to have been a local fight in which one party found its Sebastopol in the local store.

Seiad Valley, sy-ad' [Siskiyou]. Apparently of Yurok Indian origin and used since the 1850's; often spelled Sciad.

Seigler Springs, seeg'-ler [Lake]. Named in the early 1870's for the discoverer and owner, Thomas Sigler.

Selma [Fresno]. The station was named in 1880, at Leland Stanford's request, for the daughter of Max Gruenberg.

Sequoia, se-kwoi′-a. Stephan Endlicher, Austrian scholar, described the California redwood in 1847 and named it for Sequoyah (George Gist), creator of the Cherokee alphabet. The name was later applied to the Big Tree of the Sierra. The national park was named in 1890, the forest in 1908.

Serra. *See* Junipero Serra.

Sespe, ses′-pee [Ventura]. Repeatedly mentioned in mission records and recorded with the present spelling in 1824. It is Chumash Indian and is said to mean 'knee pan.'

Shafter [Kern]. Named in 1914 in memory of William ("Pecos Bill") Shafter, commander of the U. S. forces in Cuba during the Spanish-American War.

Shasta. The mountain preserves the name of Indians who once inhabited the region north of it. Their name was mentioned as early as 1814 and appeared with many spellings. In 1827 Peter Ogden bestowed the form Sastise upon a peak and river not definitely identified; in 1841 the name was fixed on the mountain and river now called Shasta. The county, one of the original twenty-seven, was named in 1850, the national forest in 1905, the dam in 1937.

Shaver Lake [Fresno]. The name was recorded as Saver and Saver's Peak by the Whitney Survey on its maps of 1873, and was probably changed in the early 1890's when C. B. Shaver built a sawmill here.

Shoshone, shoh-shoh′-nee [Inyo]. The station, named in the early 1900's, seems to be the only place in California named for the widespread family of Shoshonean Indians.

Sierra, see-ehr′-a. In Spanish times any two or more peaks in a row were called *sierra.* The term has survived in this sense in Los Angeles, Santa Cruz, and San Mateo counties. In Riverside and Orange counties the names come from two land grants of 1846. The county in the northern Sierra Nevada was named in 1852.

Sierra Madre [Los Angeles]. The town was named in the 1880's after the Sierra Madre (mother range), a term loosely applied since 1775 to the mountain chains of Los Angeles and San Bernardino counties because the Sierra Nevada and the Coast Ranges seem to spring from them.

Sierra Nevada. A descriptive Spanish name for a mountain range covered with snow. It was applied to the Santa Lucia Mountains by Cabrillo in 1542, and appears on the maps of the following centuries for various points and mountains along the coast. The range which now bears the name was first called Sierra Nevada by Font in 1776. The Frémont-Preuss map of 1845 was influential in fixing that name upon the range and eliminating Snowy Mountains, California Range, and other contenders. *See* Nevada.

Signal Hill [Los Angeles]. When the Coast Survey established the Los Angeles Base Line in 1889–1890 a signal was erected on the highest point of Los Cerritos. Thus the eminence (and the town after the discovery of oil) became known by the present name.

Silliman, Mount [Sequoia N. P.]. Named in 1864 by the Whitney Survey for Benjamin Silliman, professor of chemistry at Yale University.

Silverado. The name was coined in analogy to Eldorado and is found in several counties. The canyon in Orange County was named when silver was discovered there in the 1870's. Silverado [Napa] is the scene of Robert Louis Stevenson's *Silverado Squatters.*

Simi, sim-ee' [Ventura]. Probably from a Chumash Indian designation for 'place' or 'village.' Recorded with the present spelling as early as 1795.

Sisar [Ventura]. Creek and peak are named for a Chumash village, *Sisa,* mentioned in mission records as early as 1807.

Siskiyou. A mountain pass was given this name after Alexander R. McLeod of the Hudson's Bay Company lost a horse when going through it in 1828. *Siskiyou* ('bob-tailed horse' in the Cree Indian language) had been taken over by the Chinook Jargon, trade language of the Oregon Territory. The county was named in 1852.

Sisquoc, siss'-kwahk [Santa Barbara]. Probably a Chumash Indian name, meaning 'quail.' In 1845 the name is recorded in the title of a land grant. In 1887 it was applied to the station of the Pacific Coast R.R.

Sites [Colusa]. Named in 1887 for John H. Sites, landholder.

Six Rivers National Forest. Named by the Forest Service in 1946 because the forest embraces the watersheds of Smith, Klamath, Trinity, Mad, Van Duzen, and Eel rivers.

Ski Heil Peak [Lassen N. P.]. The German and Swiss salutation among skiers was applied to the mountain in 1937.

Smith River [Del Norte]. Jedediah Smith's name was applied in 1828 to the lower Klamath. It was transferred to the present river in 1851.

Sobrante [Contra Costa]. The town is in the Sobrante grant of 1841. *Sobrante* means 'surplus land.'

Solano, so-lah′-noh. The mission was named San Francisco Solano on July 4, 1823, and the last part of the name was given to one of the original twenty-seven counties in 1850. Solano was a chief of the Suisun Indians who had been named for the famous apostle of South America.

Soledad, sol′-e-dad. The Spanish word for 'solitude' was repeatedly used for place names and has survived in several localities. The names in San Diego County go back to an Indian rancheria, so named in 1776. The pass in Los Angeles County was likewise named after an Indian village, recorded in 1838. The name in Monterey County, however, was applied by the Portolá expedition in 1769 because the name of an Indian sounded to them like "Soledad." The mission was founded in 1791.

Solvang [Santa Barbara]. The name ('sunny meadow' in Danish) was given to the Danish American colony in 1910.

Somis [Ventura]. Applied to the railroad station in 1899. A rancheria, *Somes,* was mentioned as early as 1795.

Sonoma, so-noh′-ma. The name is derived from the Wintun word for 'nose.' It might have been first applied to an Indian chief with a big nose or to an orographic feature which resembled a nose. The Indians were mentioned as Sonomas in 1815. The town was founded by Vallejo in 1835, and the county was established and named in 1850.

Sonora, so-nor′-a [Tuolumne]. The mining camp of 1848 was known as Sonoranian Camp because of the presence of many Mexican miners from the province of Sonora. The present form came into use in 1850.

Soquel [Santa Cruz]. A *Rio de Zoquel* is mentioned in mission records in 1807. The name was probably derived from that of a Costanoan Indian village. In 1833 it was applied to the Soquel land grant.

Spadra [Los Angeles]. Named in the 1850's after Spadra Bluffs, Arkansas, former home of a settler.

Spaulding Lake [Nevada]. The reservoir was created in 1892 and named for "Uncle" John Spaulding, a former well-known stagecoach driver.

Squaw. The word is an anglicized version of an Algonkian Indian term meaning 'woman.' It has spread over the length of the United States and has been a favorite place name in California since the gold-rush days. About 200 valleys, creeks, canyons, and hollows are so named.

Stanford University. The university was established in 1885 by Leland Stanford and his wife. It was named Leland Stanford Junior University in memory of their son, who had died the preceding year. Mount Stanford and Mounts Crocker, Hopkins, and Huntington in Fresno and Mono counties were named in 1909 for the "Big Four" of the Central Pacific. Mount Stanford in Kings Canyon N. P. was named for the University.

Stanislaus, stan'-is-law, stan'-is-loss. Apparently applied to the river after 1829 for Estanislao, an Indian chief named for a Polish saint. The present spelling was used by Frémont in 1844 and applied to the county in 1854.

Starr King, Mount [Yosemite N. P.]. Applied by the Whitney Survey in memory of the Rev. Thomas Starr King (1824–1864), who helped to keep California in the Union.

Stinson Beach [Marin]. For Nathan H. Stinson, settler of 1866.

Stockton [San Joaquin]. The place was settled in 1844 by Charles M. Weber and was given its present name after Commodore Robert F. Stockton had taken possession of California for the United States in 1846.

Stovepipe Wells [Death Valley]. The two springs of good water were once protected by stovepipes.

Sugarloaf. About a hundred hills and mountains are so called because they resemble an old-fashioned sugar loaf.

Suisun Bay, su-soon′ [Solano]. The name is from the Wintun Indian rancheria mentioned with various spellings after 1806. The *Estero de los Suisunes* is recorded in 1811.

Sunol, su-nohl′ [Alameda]. Antonio Suñol, a native of Spain, came to California in 1818 and was an owner of Rancho El Valle de San Jose, granted in 1839.

Sur, sûr [Monterey]. The names, meaning 'south' [of Monterey], go back to Alvarado's land grant of 1834, El Sur.

Susanville [Lassen]. Susan was the daughter of Isaac Roop, who settled in the region in 1853 and was recorder of the "Territory of Nataqua," formed in 1856.

Sutil Island [Los Angeles]. The name applied by the Coast Survey for the ship *Sutil* of the Spanish expedition to Alaska in 1792, was approved by the Geographic Board in 1938.

Sutter. The name of the county, the fort, and a number of geographic features commemorates John A. Sutter, a German Swiss pioneer of 1839, who established the first colony in the interior central valley, Nueva (New) Helvetia, and erected the now famous landmark, Sutter's Fort, in Sacramento.

Taboose Pass [Inyo]. *Taboose,* the Indian name for an edible ground nut which was found along what is now called Division Creek, was first applied to the creek, then to the pass.

Taft [Kern]. The post office was established in 1909 and named for the newly elected President, William H. Taft.

Tahoe, tah′-hoh, **Lake.** The lake was discovered by Frémont and called first Mountain Lake, then Lake Bonpland. In 1852 it was named Lake Bigler, for the newly elected governor of California, John Bigler. This was made official by the legislature in 1870, but during the Civil War the name Tahoe had come into use, sponsored by Northern sympathizers, who resented Bigler's Southern affiliations. It was not until 1945 that the legislature changed the name officially. The national forest was named in 1906. The name is derived from the Washoe Indian *da'au,* 'lake.'

Tahquitz [Riverside]. The name is derived from the name of the bad spirit of the Cahuilla Indians. The *Tahquitz* or

Tahkoosh dwells in the San Jacinto Mountains and manifests itself as a meteor.

Tajiguas [Santa Barbara]. Creek and settlement derive the name from that of a Chumash Indian village. *Tayiyas* was another Indian word, mentioned in 1800, for 'islay,' the holly-leaved wild cherry.

Tallac [El Dorado]. The name probably signifies 'large mountain.' Both the peak and "Lucky" Baldwin's Tallac House on Lake Tahoe were mentioned in the middle 1870's.

Tamalpais, tam'-al-py'-is, **Mount** [Marin]. The Tamals were Indians living in what is now Marin County. *Pais* is said to be their word for 'mountain.' The name probably referred to the people living at the foot of the mountain. In the early 1840's the name Tamalpaiz was applied to the mountain itself. *See* Tomales.

Tanforan, tan-for-an' [San Mateo]. Station and race track were named for owners of the land in 1868.

Tassajara, tass-a-har'-a. *Tasajera* is a Spanish American word for 'a place where meat is cured' and was repeatedly used as a place name.

Tecate [San Diego]. The name is mentioned as that of an Indian rancheria in 1830 and as a rancho in 1833. It may come from the Mexican *atecate, atl* meaning 'water.'

Tecolote. The word, meaning 'twisted bill' in Mexican, designates a small owl; it is found as a place name in San Diego, Santa Barbara, and Riverside counties.

Tecopa [Inyo]. The mining camp was named for an Indian chief, who later demanded $200 for the use of his name. The name was transferred to the railroad station in 1908.

Tehachapi, te-hat'-cha-pee [Kern]. The Indian name for the creek, *Tah-ee-chay-pah,* was recorded in 1853 and was applied to the pass in the same year. The present spelling was used in 1863, and in 1876 the Southern Pacific transferred the name from the old wagon route to the railroad pass.

Tehama, te-hay'-ma. The asserted native Indian origin of the name has not yet been proved. The word may come from the Mexican *tejamanil,* 'shingle.' The town was named before 1849, the county in 1856.

Tehipite, teh-hip′-i-tee [Kings Canyon N. P.]. Probably of Mono Indian origin, meaning 'high rock.'

Tejon Canyon, te-hohn′ [Kern]. The name *Cañada del Tejon* (badger valley) was given to the canyon in 1806 because a military expedition found a dead badger at the entrance. In 1843 the name was given to a land grant. Later the pass and the southern tip of Tulare Valley became known as Tejon. **Tejon Pass** [Los Angeles]. In 1853 the Pacific Railroad Survey transferred the name from the old pass.

Telegraph Hill [San Francisco]. The arrival of ships in the Golden Gate was signaled from the hill after 1846.

Telescope Peak [Death Valley]. The peak was named in 1861 because of the wide, clear view from it.

Temecula, te-mek′-yoo-la [San Diego, Riverside]. An Indian rancheria was mentioned as *Temeca* in 1797 and as *Temecula* in 1820. *Temet* is 'sun' in Luiseño Indian.

Temescal, tem-es-kal′. The word is found in place names in various parts of the state. It was derived from the Aztec *temascal* (bathhouse) and was applied to the primitive Indian sweat houses found in California.

Tenaya, teh-ny′-a [Yosemite N. P.]. The lake was named in 1851, for Ten-ei-ya, the Indian chief of Yosemite Valley.

Tennessee Cove [Marin]. The steamer *Tennessee,* fragments of which are still visible, was wrecked here in 1853.

Tepusquet, tep′-us-ke [Santa Barbara]. This Mexican word meaning 'copper coin' was the name of a land grant, 1837.

Tequesquite. The name appears in several places. It is derived from the Mexican word for 'efflorescent rock.'

Terwah Creek [Del Norte]. A Yurok Indian village at the mouth of the creek, *Ter-war,* was mentioned in the 1850's.

Thousand Palms [Riverside]. As in Thousand Oaks, Lakes, etc., the number means 'many' and is applied to the largest group of Washingtonia palms found in California.

Throop Peak, troop [Los Angeles]. Named by the Forest Service for Amos G. Throop, founder of Throop University, now the California Institute of Technology.

Tia Juana, tee′-a wah′-na [San Diego]. Doubtless an Indian name, recorded after 1829 and usually spelled Tiajuan, though the name even in Mexican times was changed by folk etymology to Tia Juana (Aunt Jane).

Tiburon, ti-bur-on' [Marin]. *Punta de Tiburon* (shark's point) is mentioned in 1823. The post office is listed in 1887.

Tierra. The Spanish word for 'land' or 'earth' is found as a place name in many combinations.

Tinemaha [Inyo]. The peak was named by early settlers for a Piute Indian chief, Tinemaha, or Tinemakar.

Tinkers Knob [Placer]. Named for a rough, hard-driving teamster, whose nose resembled the knob.

Tocaloma [Marin]. Named after a Miwok rancheria; the second element contains the Indian root meaning 'place.'

Toiyabe National Forest. Named in 1907 after the Toiyabe Mountains in Nevada. Toiyabe is said to mean 'big hills.'

Tolenas, to-lee'-nas [Solano]. The Tolenas, or Tolenos, Indians are mentioned in records of Mission San Francisco Solano in 1824.

Toluca [Los Angeles]. An Aztec name transferred from Mexico.

Tomales, to-mah'-les [Marin]. The name was applied by the Spaniards in the 1830's and, like Tamalpais, refers to the Tamal Indians living in the district. It is possible that the Mexican word *tamal* is the source of the name.

Topango [Los Angeles]. The name is from the Shoshonean Indian dialect. A land grant Topanga Malibu was made in 1805; a *Punta de Topanga* is recorded in 1839.

Topa Topa Mountain, toh'-pah [Ventura]. A Chumash Indian name derived from *Topotopow* or *Si-toptopo.* The derivation from Spanish *topo* (mole) is not impossible.

Torquemada, Mount [Santa Catalina Island]. Probably named for Juan de Torquemada, who published *Monarchia Indiana* in 1615.

Toro. The Spanish word for 'bull' is found in a number of place names, some of which date from Spanish times. The name in Monterey County is mentioned as early as 1785, and an *Arroyo del Toro* is recorded in 1834. The place in Orange County was so called before 1838 because "there was a nice tame bull there."

Torrance [Los Angeles]. Planned in 1911 as a model city and named by the owner of the land, Jared S. Torrance.

Towne Pass [Inyo]. Named in 1860 for a Captain Towne, who led a party from Death Valley through this pass in 1849.

Toyon, toi'-on [Shasta]. This town and several other places in the state are named for the red-berried native shrub.

Trabuco, tra-bu'-ko [Orange]. The canyon was named by Portolá's soldiers in 1769 because they lost a blunderbuss (*trabuco*) there. *Sierra de Trabuco* is mentioned by Anza in 1775; *Cerro* (hill) *de Trabuco* is recorded in 1827; in 1841 the name was applied to a land grant.

Tracy [San Joaquin]. Named in 1878 by the Southern Pacific for one of its officials, Lathrop J. Tracy.

Tranquillon Mountain [Santa Barbara]. The name of the prominent landfall, applied about 1880 by the Coast Survey, is from an Indian name of unknown origin.

Treasure Island [San Francisco Bay]. Chosen in a contest in 1936 by the directors of the Golden Gate International Exposition as a name having good publicity value.

Tres Pinos, tres pee'-nos [San Benito]. In 1873 the Southern Pacific gave the name to the terminal of the proposed Pacheco Pass route, appropriating it from a near-by settlement which had been named for its 'three pines.'

Trevarno [Alameda]. Named after the town in Cornwall.

Trinidad [Humboldt]. The Bruno de Hezeta expedition took possession of the bay on June 11, 1775, and called it *Puerto de la Trinidad* because it was Trinity Sunday. The town was named in 1850.

Trinity. Pierson B. Reading believed that the river emptied into Trinidad Bay, and therefore applied to it in 1845 the English equivalent of the Spanish Trinidad. The county, one of the original twenty-seven, was named in 1850 and the national forest in 1905.

Triunfo [Ventura, Los Angeles]. The Portolá expedition camped probably in what is now Potrero Valley on January 13, 1770, and Crespi called the valley *El triunfo del Dulcisimo Nombre de Jesus* (The triumph of the sweet name of Jesus). Next day Crespi called an Indian rancheria in what is now Russell Valley *El triunfo de Jesus*. The abbreviated form appears in mission and land-grant papers. The settlement is shown on maps since the early 1850's.

Trona [San Bernardino]. The name is derived from the mineral, a variety of potash, found in the lake.

Truckee [Placer, Nevada]. The river and lake (now Donner Lake) were named for an Indian who piloted part of the Stevens party across the Sierra in 1844.

Tucki Mountain [Death Valley]. Named in 1909. *Tucki* is the Shoshonean Indian word for sheep.

Tujunga, ta-hung'-ga [Los Angeles]. An Indian rancheria, *Tuyunga*, was noted in 1795, and a *sierra* called Tujunga in 1822. In 1840 the name appears in a land grant.

Tulare, too-lair'-ee, too-lair'; **Tule**, too'-lee. The Mexican words for 'cattail' or 'bulrush,' and for places where the *tule* grows, are found in marshy sections of the state, especially in the southern San Joaquin Valley. *Los Tulares* in this district were mentioned in 1773; *Tulareños*, the collective name for the Indians of the valley, appears after 1800; Tulare Lake and River since the early 1840's. Tulare County was named in 1852.

Tulucay Creek [Napa]. The name is derived from the Pomo Indian *tuluka* (red). It was applied to an Indian village in 1824, and in 1841 to a land grant, Tulucay.

Tumco [Imperial]. The name was coined in 1910 from the initials of *The United Mines Company*.

Tunemah [Fresno]. The Chinese who were employed as cooks by early prospectors and sheepherders used all sorts of cuss words in describing the roughness of this trail. The most common, *tunemah*, finally gave the name to the pass.

Tuolumne, twah'-lu-me. The river was named for Indians of the district. A rancheria called *Taulamne* and *Tahualamne* was noted in 1806 on the Stanislaus River. It is probably a Yokuts Indian word, meaning 'cave people,' i.e., those who dwell in the rocks and recesses by the rivers. A *Rio de los Towalumnes* is shown on the Frémont-Preuss map of 1848. The present spelling was used for the county in 1850.

Turlock [Stanislaus]. When the railroad reached the place in 1871, John W. Mitchell modestly declined to have the station on his property named for him and suggested the present name, after Turlough in county Mayo, Ireland.

Twentynine Palms [San Bernardino]. Named Palm Springs during Railroad Survey, 1855; later Twentynine Palms Spring. Changed to present form in 1927.

Tyndall, Mount [Inyo, Tulare]. Named in 1864 by the Whitney Survey for John Tyndall, British scientist and alpinist.

Ubehebe, yoo-bee-hee'-bee [Death Valley]. The name for the peak is mentioned in 1883; it is a Shoshonean Indian word but the meaning is not known.

Ukiah, yoo-ky'-a [Mendocino]. The name, recorded as Yokaya in 1845, has been spelled Ukiah since 1856 when the town was founded; it probably means 'south valley.'

Umunhum, Mount [Santa Clara]. Probably named for the hummingbird, in Indian mythology one of the creators of the world.

Usal, yoo'-sal [Mendocino]. Probably the Pomo Indian word *yoshol,* containing the stem *yo* (south).

Uvas, oo'-vas, yoo'-vas. The Spanish name for grapes is preserved in a number of place names, all apparently referring to the presence of native wild grapes.

Vaca, Vacaville [Napa, Solano]. The names commemorate the Vaca family who came from New Mexico in 1841 and settled in this district a few years later.

Vallecito. The Spanish for 'little valley' is preserved in place names in San Diego, San Benito, and Calaveras counties.

Vallejo, va-lay'-oh [Solano]. Laid out in 1850 by M. G. Vallejo, long the leading pioneer on the northern frontier. It was the capital of the state in 1851 and 1852.

Van Duzen River [Humboldt, Trinity]. The name was given by the Gregg party in January, 1850, for one of its members. It was recorded as Vandusen's Fork in 1853.

Van Nuys [Los Angeles]. Named for Isaac N. Van Nuys, southern California pioneer of the 1870's.

Vasquez Rocks, vas-kwez' [Los Angeles]. The notorious bandit Tiburcio Vasquez presumably had his hideout here in the 1870's.

Ventura, ven-toor'-a. The name is an abbreviation of San Buenaventura, the name of the mission established in 1782. The county has been Ventura from its inception in 1872; the railroad station was San Buenaventura until 1888, the post office until 1891.

Verdugo, ver-doo'-go [Los Angeles]. The name commemorates José María Verdugo, a corporal in the San Gabriel mission guard and grantee of one of the first land grants in Upper California, dated October 20, 1784.

Vernal Fall [Yosemite N. P.]. The Latin for 'spring' was applied in 1851; the atmosphere "suggested the sensation of spring."

Victorville [San Bernardino]. Named Victor in 1885, for J. N. Victor, superintendent of the California Southern R.R.; changed to the present form in 1901.

Vina. The Spanish word *viña* for 'vineyard' is often used for place names.

Visalia [Tulare]. Named in 1852 by Nat Vise after Visalia, Kentucky, in turn named for the Vise family.

Visitacion [San Mateo, San Francisco]. The name was taken from the *Rancho Cañada de Guadalupe y la Visitacion* of 1841. A place called *la Visitacion,* where the San Francisco presidio kept livestock, was mentioned in 1798. The name itself is derived from the Visitation of the Blessed Virgin Mary.

Vista [San Diego]. When the Santa Fe built across the old Buena Vista (good view) Rancho in 1890 it named one station Buena Vista. When in 1908 a name was needed for another station, the old one was called Buena and the new one Vista.

Vizcaino, vis-kay'-noh [Mendocino]. The name of the cape commemorates Sebastián Vizcaíno, the explorer of 1602–1603.

Vogelsang [Yosemite N. P.]. Named in 1907 for Charles A. Vogelsang, officer of the State Fish and Game Commission.

Wahtoke [Fresno]. An Indian village or tribe on Kings River was mentioned as Wattokes in 1857; in the Fresno reservation as Wartokes in 1861. The Santa Fe station was named in 1910. The name may come from the Yokuts Indian *watak* (pine nut).

Walker. Several geographic features in California bear this name. **Walker Pass** [Kern] and **Walker River** [Mono] were named by Frémont, for Joseph R. Walker of Tennessee, one of the great trail blazers, who came to California in 1833 and returned to the Rocky Mountains in 1834 over the Sierra pass which now bears his name. He led a part of the Chiles party into California in 1843, and was Frémont's guide in 1845–1846. **Walker Lake** and **Creek** in Mono County were named for William J. Walker, who settled there in 1880, but the names are often associated with the famous Walker.

Walnut. A number of places have been named for the most widely cultivated of the nut family. Walnut Creek [Contra Costa] goes back to Spanish times: *un arroyo que llaman los nogales* (a creek called the walnut trees) was mentioned in 1810. Walnut Grove [Sacramento] was named in the early 1860's, and Walnut [Los Angeles] was changed in 1912 from Lemon.

Walteria [Los Angeles]. The post office was named in 1926 for Captain Walters, who had built the first hotel here.

Warner Springs [San Diego]. Jonathan Warner, an immigrant of 1831, received the Agua Caliente grant in 1844. The ranch became a famous station on the emigrant trail.

Wasco [Kern]. The name of the Oregon county was applied to the Santa Fe station in 1898 by a former Oregonian.

Waterman Canyon [San Bernardino]. Named for Robert W. Waterman, governor of California, 1887–1891.

Watkins, Mount [Yosemite N. P.]. Named for Carleton E. Watkins, whose photographs of Yosemite Valley in the 1860's received wide attention.

Watsonville [Santa Cruz]. The post office was established in 1854 and named for Judge John H. Watson, owner of the land.

Wawona [Mariposa]. The hotel was built in 1875 and named Wawona. The word means 'big tree' in the local Indian dialect; it was formed in imitation of the hoot of the owl, the guardian spirit of the trees.

Weed [Siskiyou]. Named in 1900 for Abner Weed, county supervisor; state senator, 1907–1909.

Weimar, wee'-mer [Placer]. The post office was named in memory of "old Weimah," a colorful Indian chief of the 1850's. In 1886 it was recorded with the present spelling, like that of the German city.

Weitchpec, wich'-pek [Humboldt]. The name probably means 'meeting of the waters'; it was mentioned in 1852 for an Indian language group at the confluence of Klamath and Trinity rivers.

Weott [Humboldt]. Recorded in 1851 as Wee-yot, the Indian name for the Eel River and the Indians on its shore.

Wheeler. The peak in Mono and the ridge in Kern County commemorate Lieutenant George M. Wheeler, in the 1870's in charge of the survey west of the 100th meridian.

Whipple Mountains [San Bernardino]. Named in 1858 for Lieutenant A. W. Whipple, a member of the Mexican Boundary Commission and the Pacific Railroad Survey.

Whitney, Mount [Tulare, Inyo]. The highest peak of the United States (outside of Alaska) was named in July, 1864, by a party of the Whitney Survey for their chief, Josiah Dwight Whitney, State Geologist from 1860 to 1874.

Whittier [Los Angeles]. Named in 1887 by Quakers, for John Greenleaf Whittier, poet and reformer.

Williamson, Mount [Inyo]. Named by the Whitney Survey in 1864 for Lieutenant Robert S. Williamson, who was in charge of the Pacific Railroad Survey in the 1850's.

Willits [Mendocino]. Named for Hiram Willits, who owned land here in the 1850's.

Willows [Glenn]. The town was laid out in 1876, and named after Willow Slough, east of the site.

Wilmington [Los Angeles]. The original name, New San Pedro, was changed in 1863 to Wilmington, after the city in Delaware, former home of the founder, Phineas Banning.

Wilson, Mount [Los Angeles]. Named for Benjamin D. ("Don Benito") Wilson, first mayor of Los Angeles under American rule, who built a burro trail up the mountain in 1864.

Winchell, Mount [Inyo]. For Alexander Winchell, until 1891 professor of geology at the University of Michigan.

Wingate Pass [San Bernardino]. Possibly named in memory of Major Benjamin Wingate, who died in 1862.

Wolfskill [Solano]. Named for William and John Wolfskill, pioneers of 1838, grantee and occupant, respectively, of the land grant Rio de los Putos, 1842.

Woodland [Yolo]. The popular American place name was applied to the post office in 1859.

Ydalpom [Shasta]. Named after the Wintun Indian village, *Wai-dal-pom* (place lying north).

Yerba Buena. The Spanish name, 'good herb,' for the white-flowered wild mint, is preserved in the name of the island in San Francisco Bay, called *Isla de Alcatraces* in 1775 and *Ysla de la Yerba Buena* in 1795. The site of what is now downtown San Francisco was known as Yerba Buena when it was settled in 1835. *See* San Francisco.

Yermo [San Bernardino]. The appropriate name, 'desert' in Spanish, was given to the post office in 1908.

Yolla Bolly [Trinity]. *Yola* means 'snow' and *bally* 'mountain' in Wintun Indian. *See* Bally.

Yolo. The county, one of the original twenty-seven, was named in 1850; the town was Cacheville until 1854. *Rancho del Ioleo* is shown on a map of 1844, south of present Cache Creek. Yolo, mentioned as captain of an Indian rancheria at Tomales Bay in 1810, probably has nothing to do with this name.

Yorba Linda [Orange]. A real-estate name, combining the names of two near-by places, Yorba and Olinda. The Yorbas were one of the oldest and most respected pioneer families of the district.

Yosemite, yo-sem'-i-tee. The name Yosemity was applied to the valley when it was discovered by the Mariposa Battalion in March, 1851, but has been used with the present spelling since 1852. The name meant 'the Grizzlies' or 'the Killers' and was applied by the neighboring tribes to the valley Indians because of their lawless character.

Yountville [Napa]. Named about 1867 for George C. Yount of North Carolina, immigrant of 1831, who settled in the vicinity in 1836.

Yreka, wy-ree'-ka [Siskiyou]. The city was named by act of the legislature in 1852 after the Indian name of Mount Shasta (Wai-i-ka). The intended spelling was Wyreka, and the present version is due to a clerical error.

Yuba. The name Yubu was applied to the river by Sutter in 1839 or 1840, after the Maidu Indian village, opposite the mouth of the river. The county, one of the original twenty-seven, was named in 1850.

Yucca. Several varieties of the plant, including the Joshua tree, *Yucca brevifolia,* have provided a number of place names.

Yucaipa, yoo-ky'-pa [San Bernardino]. A Shoshonean Indian place name, recorded with the present spelling in 1841. The word means 'wet or marshy land,' the last syllable doubtless from *pah,* 'water.'

Yuma [Imperial]. The fort was established in 1850 and named for the Indian tribe on the banks of the Colorado. The Yumas were mentioned about 1700, and the meaning of the name is probably 'sons of the river.'

Zabriskie Point [Inyo]. Named for Christian B. Zabriskie, of the Pacific Coast Borax Company.

Zaca [Santa Barbara]. A Chumash Indian rancheria, Saca, was mentioned in 1806, and the present spelling was applied to a land grant in 1838.

Zanja, Zanjon. The Spanish words meaning 'ditch,' 'drain,' 'channel' were often used in Spanish times, and have survived as place names in Alameda, San Bernardino, and Santa Barbara counties.

Zurich [Inyo]. The name of the Swiss city was applied to the station in 1913 because of the Alpine scenery to the west.

NOTES

NOTES

NOTES

NOTES

NOTES

NOTES

NOTES